A Lantern in the Wind

A Lantern
in the Wind

THE LIFE OF
Mary Ellen Chase

BY ELIENNE SQUIRE

Fithian Press

SANTA BARBARA · 1995

Design and typography by Jim Cook
Cover photo: Maine Women Writers Collection, Westbrook College,
Portland, Maine

Published by Fithian Press, P.O. Box 1525, Santa Barbara, CA 93102

LIBRARY OF CONGRESS CATALOGING-IN-PUBLICATION DATA
Squire, Elienne
        A lantern in the wind : the life of Mary Ellen Chase / by
Elienne Squire.
              p.   cm.
        Includes bibliographical references.
        ISBN 1-56474-132-X
        1. Chase, Mary Ellen, 1887-1973–Biography. 2. Women authors,
American–20th century–Biography. 3. English teachers–United
States–Biography. 4. Feminists–United States–Biography.
5. Lesbians–United States–Biography. I. Title.
PS3505.H48Z87   1995
813'.52—dc20   94-46762
    [B]   CIP

What is man?
A passing wayfarer, a guest on earth?
What is man's place on earth?
A lantern in the wind.

—ALCUIN, *Questions and Answers*

Contents

Acknowledgements

Essential background sources for this biography include: Boston University Special Collections, Dr. Howard Gottlieb, Director, Karen Mix, Archivist; Bowdoin College Special Collections; Colby College Special Collections, Patience Anne Lenk, Director; Columbia University Rare Books, Bernard Chrystal, Director; University of Maine at Orono, Fogler Library, Muriel Sanford, Archivist; University of Minnesota Rare Books, Lois Hendrickson, Director, Penelope Krosch, Assistant Director. Invaluable assistance was made possible through these sources at Smith College: Smith College Rare Books; Sophia Smith Collections, Maida Goodwin, Archives Specialist; Smith College Archives, Margery Sly, Archivist; Smith College Development Office, Charlotte Heartt, Director.

I am especially grateful to supportive family members who urged me to see this project through: Rebecca and Gary Guenther, Jon Squire and Megan McKeon, David Hirshey, and my pro bono editor and sweetest inspiration, Susan Squire. My grandchildren, Aaron and Sarah Guenther and Emily Hirshey, afforded moments of light and fun. And my mother, Esther Ziskind Weltman, a loyal Smith alumna who died before publication of the book, was my mainstay during some very trying times. Perhaps she knows, and is glad.

Introduction

In 1987, to mark the centenary of Mary Ellen Chase's birth, I wrote a reflective essay to honor this remarkable woman who had a great impact on a generation of students. The article, printed in the *Smith Alumnae Quarterly*, elicited so many enthusiastic replies that I was prompted to learn more about Chase. What made her so special, when most of her colleagues had slipped into oblivion? After four decades her students recall her vividly: her wisdom, kindness, support, and personal concern. Chase truly cared for her fledglings, what they would glean from the classroom and how they would apply this knowledge in the world at large. She firmly believed that each individual had an obligation to the community, and she was acutely aware of the inseparable relationship between learning and life. Her associate Daniel Aaron observed that she had a "sweetness, generosity, romantic girlish impulse in her responses and compassion for others."

I met Chase in 1943 when she spoke to the junior class at Classical High School in Springfield, Massachusetts. After the lecture, I summoned up the courage to introduce myself. When she asked me why I chose Smith, I told her that she was the reason. I asked meekly whether I could be in her freshman English class, a group of twenty personally selected students.

She said she would honor my request if I received A's in all senior English courses. She kept her promise.

At first, I had mixed feelings about Chase. I was captivated by her charm and vitality, but intimidated by the high standards she set. During my college years, I knew her outside of the classroom as a highly principled, dedicated scholar, a ready listener and a valued confidante. In 1947 I was a member of her Bible class; it was at this time that Chase and my parents became acquainted.

In March 1948, during a lecture to a group of ministers on the Bible and modern Jewish preaching, Rabbi Abraham Feldman of Temple Beth Israel in Hartford, Connecticut, censured Chase's study, *The Bible and the Common Reader,* for its "sneers and flippant dismissals." A local newspaper printed excerpts of his talk, and my father, an attorney of strong moral fiber, was offended by Feldman's harsh accusations. He knew that Chase was sincere in her attempt to dispel the barriers of intolerance at the college. He wrote the Rabbi, stating that his daughter had learned more in one semester of the Bible course than in all her years at religious school. I gave Chase a copy of this letter and she was deeply touched; she told my father that he was "an Amos come to my rescue."

I spent many stimulating hours in Chase's cozy living room, enjoying her freshly brewed coffee and savory date-nut bread. On several occasions, I drove her to Springfield where she spoke to enamored Smith alumnae. Despite her apparent self-confidence, I remember how nervous she was; to allay her anxiety, she smoked a cigarette in an obscure area of the parking lot.

Chase's life was not an easy one. As a child, she felt rejected and unloved, inferior in every respect to her sisters, Mildred and Edith. She considered herself slow and stupid, always seeking approval, but rarely receiving it. She thought she was a failure in the opinion of her father, whom she loved in spite of his difficult temperament. When she left home to begin her teaching career, she felt inadequate and undeserving.

During her years of recuperation from tuberculosis in Montana, without the support of family and friends, she could have surrendered, but she persevered; through sheer determination, she composed her first three books. This was a desolate time in her life, but through solitude, she acquired a personal dignity, self-possession, self-reliance, and patience.

The road to success was a hard upward climb. Many of her early stories were written for financial reasons, to supplement her income and assist her widowed mother and younger siblings. In 1926, when she came to Smith College, she began writing books which established her as a leading regional novelist. *Mary Peters* (1934) is the first of two novels dealing with conditions of change as Maine's maritime power was threatened by the onset of the Industrial Revolution. *Silas Crockett,* completed the following year, was hailed as Chase's most significant contribution to the social and cultural history of her native state, and revealed her as a master of the family saga. In *Windswept* (1941), her most famous and most personal novel, she incorporates her love for the land, for roots, into the very meaning of the book. This engrossing family chronicle became a best seller and made her rich and famous.

Three of Chase's pivotal works recapture her Maine girlhood and experience as an apprentice teacher and graduate student. *A Goodly Heritage, A Goodly Fellowship,* and *The White Gate* are the best introductions to Chase as an individual and as an artist. They are in the mainstream of her writing, rich in terms of rhythmic structure and narrative skill. These works take their place among the most distinguished of American reminiscences and present an accurate picture of life in a small New England coastal town.

Chase wrote thirty volumes of fiction, essays, biography, literary criticism, and a provocative series of Bible studies. Her prolific output reflects a wide range of knowledge as well as exceptional creative power. Her belief in man's invincibility and endurance constitute the center of her drama and the major metaphor of her vision. As a Humanist, Chase believed in the transcendency of spirit and intellect; she rejected all theories absolving man from accountability for his actions. Her prevailing tenet was that mind and spirit supercede matter, render man unique and make him the master of his destiny.

Chase found her greatest happiness at Windswept, in Northampton, and in Cambridge, England. She found her staunchest ally in her live-in companion, Eleanor Duckett, who never failed her. Duckett was good-natured, serene and seemingly detached from the ironies and tragedies of life, except in moments of compassion for others.

Chase was identified with Smith College for over thirty years, enhancing its prestige and deriving joy from her work there. She was one of the stellar figures in the annals of the college, whose purpose she helped to define. She revered President Neilson; he encouraged students and faculty to cultivate within themselves the desire to be alone so that they might perceive their "noisy days and years as but moments in the being of the eternal Silence."

ELIENNE SQUIRE

Cambridge, Massachusetts
August 1994

I.

The Early Years

CHAPTER ONE

Blue Hill Beginnings
1762-1885

The coast of Maine from Kittery Point to Eastport extends for 1,500 miles; one of the most imposing sights is that section between Frenchman's and Penobscot Bays. Blue Hill, situated fourteen miles from Ellsworth, is a panoramic sweep of land with Camden Hills to the west, Mount Desert to the east, and the sea to the south. Small fields and rolling hills stretch backwards and upwards until they merge into an uneven skyline of pines and firs. The bay, approximately ten miles wide and equally as long, is dotted with rocky inlets. It is separated from the coast by a chain of larger islands, the most prominent of which contain the fishing villages of Swans Island and Frenchboro. The name evolved from the low spruce trees that encircle the cove and lend a blue-green tint to the surrounding hills.

Blue Hill retains much of its original charm and natural beauty. In over 230 years of existence the population has rarely exceeded 1,500. The village is remote and sequestered among the high hills, and at the end of the land-locked harbor the old houses stand on elm-shaded streets, the blacksmith shop overlooks the millbrook, and the chimes of the two white churches ring at nine and eleven on Sunday mornings. Many traditions are observed today: the villagers fashion tissue and crepe May baskets to hang on doorknobs, church suppers retain their popularity, and on Memorial Day the children place fresh flowers on the soldiers' graves.

The village has a long and honorable history. Formerly called East Boston, it was founded in 1762 after the termination of the English, French and Indian Wars. Blue Hill's first dwellers were farmers, fishermen and sailors of middle-class British descent. They were attracted to the region by the navigable waters of the Kennebec and Penobscot Rivers and the nearby Portland harbor. Eager to acquire sufficient acreage to sustain themselves and their families, in January 1762 these settlers petitioned the General Court of Massachusetts for a tract of arable land between Passamaquoddy Bay and the Penobscot. Among them were John Roundy and Joseph Wood, Mary Ellen Chase's great-great-great-grandfather. Wood's daughter Edith was the first white child born on the shores of Blue Hill Bay.

The petitioners' appeal was granted two months later in the House of Representatives, but the final decision was delayed until the King's approval. Weary of waiting, Roundy and Wood moved to Blue Hill without permission or legal rights. A few years later they were joined by others seeking similar privileges; in less than two decades they had cleared fertile land, built homes and formed adjacent colonies. The natives married among themselves until after five generations the same genes were distributed among many families. This homogeneity resulted in a fierce resistance to any outsiders.

Two aspects of change established Blue Hill. The invasion of summer tourists, or rusticators, greatly altered the livelihood, mores and perspective of the native stock. The first wave of transients appeared around the turn of the century. They knew little of Maine history and Maine character, and had a condescending attitude which Downeasters found intolerable. Thus an insurmountable barrier arose between newcomers and natives.

The second period of modification counteracted the first. The stock market crash of 1929 and its effects wrought a widespread and salubrious change in the summer colonies along the Maine coast. The vacationers who came to Blue Hill after the economic reversal were genuinely interested in the town's welfare, and they added immeasurably to the cultural standing of the village. They contributed far more than material prosperity in return for the peace and freedom which they cherished.

In early New England large families were the norm. They not only advanced the growth of the community, but also fulfilled one's duty to God. Ten to fifteen children represented a respectable New England family; it was debatable whether those with only five or six had met their earthly obligations. Adherence to the Congregational Church was mandatory, those who defected were considered to be heretics. One of these defectors, Benjamin Lord, was Mary Chase's great-great grandfather. In 1805, after his enforced removal from Blue Hill, he became an itinerant preacher, tirelessly travelling hundreds of miles to other seacoast villages, devoting his life to the promulgation of the Baptist faith. His son, Heard Lord, born in 1806, followed his father's tradition and was a leading church figure. In his early twenties, he served as schoolmaster in the eastern Maine seacoast towns, taught singing at night and was an accomplished carpenter and shoemaker. Until his death he made his own shoes as well as those of his family.

Heard and his wife Serena had one son, John Newton Lord, born on August 23, 1834. He married Edith Wood Hinckley, the daughter of a proper Blue Hill family. Their only child, Edith Mable Lord, born on June 7, 1866, was Mary Ellen Chase's mother. Mable was nine when her mother died of consumption; three years later her father married Elizabeth Hibbard, and the couple moved to Waltham, Massachusetts.

Mable chose to remain in Blue Hill with her grandparents to continue her studies at the Academy.

In 1878, when Mable entered the Academy, female seminaries and women's colleges were gaining recognition. She witnessed the wider entrance of her sex into the teaching profession and was aware that women could surpass men academically. She was also convinced that marriage was not the only answer to a woman's happiness. After her graduation at age sixteen, Mable taught two terms of district school, receiving a salary of five dollars a week. Her proficiency in Latin earned her a job as instructor of Latin grammar and Cicero, enlightening young farmers who dreamed of Bowdoin College while they sawed and split wood. While Mable taught she studied, memorizing the orations against Cataline and the six books of the *Aeneid* with a mind so retentive that in later years she was able to assist her grandchildren with their homework.

On June 5, 1884, two days before her eighteenth birthday, Mable married Edward Everett Chase, the son of Eliza and Melatiah. Over a span of twenty-seven years they had eight children: the oldest, Mildred, was born in May 1885, shortly before her mother's nineteenth birthday; the youngest, Newton, in March 1912 as Mable approached her forty-sixth year. Mary Ellen, born in 1887, was the second Chase offspring.

The greatest single influence on Mary's life was her paternal grandmother, a woman endowed with abundant vitality and consummate charm. Her stories provided a rich harvest for fiction. Eliza Ann Wescott, the daughter of John Wescott and Eliza Lowell and the cousin of James Russell Lowell, was one of those rare individuals who seemed destined for adventure. The oldest of ten children, she was born on a barren uplands farm five miles from Blue Hill. From early childhood she displayed an ability to convert hard labor into pleasure: "I was happy as a child," she told her grandchildren. "Time never lay heavy on my hands. I never had to ask my mother what I might do. I loved hard work, for I could show how smart I was."

Eliza played a dominant role in the nurturing of her younger siblings. On her tenth birthday, when her parents went to town for provisions, she was left in charge of several of the children. By eleven o'clock she had churned and made ten pounds of butter, by noon she had fed six small Wescotts and two hired farm hands. After she washed the dishes, she cut and fashioned a new suit, coat, vest and trousers for five-year-old John. When her parents returned, John was proudly clad in his new outfit.

Every Sunday Eliza walked five miles with her sisters and brothers to and from Blue Hill's Congregational Church. Between April and November she carried her shoes and hand-knit hose; at the first sight of the church, she washed her feet and put on the stockings and shoes for the service only, trudging home barefoot. When she was fifteen, Eliza became a midwife in the village and outlying districts, a profession she had learned while assisting at the birth of her siblings. At seventeen she travelled thirty miles to Bangor in the back of an old farm wagon to master the art of dressmaking; she sewed for twenty-five cents a day for families more affluent than her own.

In April 1847, when she was twenty-two, Eliza met Melatiah Kimball Chase, sole survivor of a disastrous shipwreck that claimed the lives of thirty men, including his brother. She sang in the church choir at a memorial service for the lost crew. Melatiah was captivated by the beguiling girl, dressed in a pink calico frock and a straw bonnet adorned with pink roses. On July 16, 1849, the couple were wed in the same church. The bride wore the first silk dress she had ever owned. The handmade gown was of pearl gray taffeta with rose accents, a double skirt with hoops and bishop's sleeves and bows of rose velvet encircled her tiny waist. At her bridegroom's request she wore a gray silk bonnet with a wreath of pink roses beneath the brim. She carried his gift, an ivory-handled pink parasol that he had brought from France.

Their honeymoon was spent on Melatiah's new 1,500-ton barque, *The Bride;* its mission was to transport flour to Bermuda. They sailed from New York on August 1, 1849. After four days at sea, off Cape Hatteras, the ship encountered a blustery gale. Melatiah carried his wife onto the deck where she remained for thirty-six terrifying hours as the wind tore the rigging and heavy seas ripped her clothes. Fears of death mingled with a desire for release as wind and water lashed her chapped and burning skin. When the storm abated, the captain of a British ship launched his boats and saved the officers and crew. Eliza was too ill to witness the final destruction of *The Bride*; it was consumed by the sea less than an hour after their rescue.

Two months after the mishap, the newlyweds settled in Blue Hill. But not for long. With the insurance money, the plucky couple bought another ship, *The Eliza Ann Chase*. For twelve years they sailed together in relative safety; Eliza remained at home only for the birth of their children. Their first two were girls who died young: Abby in 1854 at age four from injuries sustained when she accidentally fell from a window; Annie in 1861 at five from diphtheria. A third daughter, Mary Dyer, known as Minnie, had a severe speech impediment caused by falling on a sharp pencil that split her palate. Despite this handicap, Minnie was a bright girl with a love of literature. She attended Mount Holyoke Seminary and married Addison Herrick, a prominent educator and probate judge.

After the exciting days at sea, Eliza found it difficult adjusting to village life. Monotony stifled her free spirit. Aware that her husband would never willingly let her out of his sight, she began to devise ingenious schemes of escape. She told him that she had detected symptoms of cancer and that she must go to Boston for treatment. Melatiah arranged for her to stay with a minister on the outskirts of the city. Lonely and anxious for her return, he wrote her a touching letter: "Stay, dear wife. Stay as long as you must. Do not worry. All is well here. The housekeeper is no good. The children cry for you and pray for you each night. I begin to feel poorly. Stay. Stay as long as you must." Eliza remained in the city until she became restless;

then, temporarily cured, she returned home laden with trunks of silk and calico.

After his retirement in 1860, Melatiah bought a grocery store and a neighborhood quarry. The same year he purchased a large, rambling house on the edge of Blue Hill Village, equipped with stables and sufficient land to retain several animals. It was there that their son Edward Everett was born; to commemorate the joyous occasion Melatiah brought elm seedlings from the mountains to shade the house and grounds. The stately trees were a landmark of the Chase residence; by the time the house was sold in 1954, it had sheltered the family for six generations.

When Melatiah died at age sixty-one on December 27, 1884, Eliza was devastated. She did not want to leave their home, nor did she want to live there alone. Edward and Mable, married for less than a year, gave up their little house and moved into hers, where all of their eight children were born. "It is not easy for your grandmother having all of us here," Mable explained to her children. It was not easy for anyone, for although Eliza's heart was broken, her spirit was not.

With the exception of the winter months spent with her daughter Minnie in Bethel, Eliza made weekly pilgrimages to her husband's grave in Seaside Cemetery. The plot was impressive in its display of Blue Hill granite; the entrance was adorned with handsome antique urns filled with fresh bouquets. Eliza often picked flowers from other gardens. An irate neighbor, whose geraniums were plucked by Eliza, complained to Edward. When he admonished his mother that she was breaking the law, she retorted, "Who, may I ask, has the right to make laws for those who have gone ahead?"

From the time of her husband's death until her own, Eliza dressed entirely in black or white. Even her handkerchiefs had wide black borders. But her wardrobe had a variety of accessories: fichus, jabots, collars, ruchings, bolts of beaded braid, and yards of Brussels lace. The prospect of her own demise was a constant concern, not because she feared a lingering illness, but simply because she thought she might not look her best at her funeral. In her bureau drawer was an elegant black satin dress wrapped in multiple layers of tissue which she had chosen for her burial. Each year she draped the gown with great solemnity on the parlor sofa to show her granddaughter Edith, whom Eliza considered a fashion expert. Eliza survived her husband by thirty years; she died at eighty-six in March 1914, one day after her beloved son's death. At her funeral she wore the shimmering black ensemble with a touch of Brussels lace, which was exactly what stylish Boston matrons were donning that spring.

CHAPTER TWO

Edward Everett Chase
1861-1914

Edward Everett Chase was born on March 19, 1861. As the youngest child and long-awaited heir, he was idolized by his mother and raised permissively. His parents were determined to give him the best possible education in preparation for a professional career. When he was eleven he went to Westbrook Academy in Portland, a grammar school modeled after the strict English convention. He was proficient in his studies, but only in the subjects he liked. At fourteen he entered the Classical Institute at Hallowell, which trained boys specifically for Bowdoin College. According to his teachers, he was not a traditional scholar, but an avid reader with a remarkable gift for memorizing dates. His behavior was often unacceptable; at the academy he was a trouble-maker and equally defiant in Blue Hill.

Edward spent the summer of 1882 in Waldoboro, reading Homer in its original version under the tutelage of a Congregational minister. That fall he entered Bowdoin; although he did not complete his studies there, his love of literature became the consuming passion of his life. History was his chief interest; he prized facts because of the opportunity they afforded for thought and reflection. In later years, he interrogated his children as to the time of great events, demanding that they memorize names and dates of all the English kings and American presidents. He insisted that they recite each list along with the counties of Maine, the countries of Asia, the Twelve Apostles according to St. Matthew, and the rulers of the Kingdom of Israel.

Shortly after his marriage, Edward joined the Ellsworth law

firm of Wiswell and King as a clerk. On his weekly jaunts between Ellsworth and Blue Hill he read voraciously; he memorized every word of Horace's *Odes* and Burke's *Orations*. He was rarely without a book in his hand; his daughter Mary remembered him as a "big, dark man, sunk in his great chair, one unquiet hand upon his forehead, the other quietly turning the pages of Creasey's *Fifteen Decisive Battles of the World* or Macauley's *History*."

Mary described her father as a fine and brilliant man. What she did not mention in any of her works was that he was an alcoholic, and this tempered her love for him. The children, who addressed him politely as "Sir," judged his moods by the nature of the recitation he mumbled as he came to breakfast. Greek hexameters indicated congeniality, Lincoln's Gettysburg Address implied that they should be unobtrusive. He was a catalog of contradictions: he encouraged his children to economize, yet he was careless with money; he expressed his admiration for mathematics, but depended on his wife for household accounting; he was forever lamenting the lack of "practical common sense," but he displayed very little; he deplored "sentimental nonsense," but all his life he was an incurable romantic.

The children regarded him as a stern, unpredictable and complex man who was mainly interested in the discipline of their minds and whose chief role was to administer punishment. The older four, Mildred, Mary, Edith, and Edward, Jr., recalled him as a rigid, restless figure who commanded respect and represented authority; the younger set, Olive, John and Virginia (excluding Newton who was only three when his father died) spent most of their childhood trying to offset their apprehensions. Virginia was twelve when her father died, and did not mourn his passing. With a kind of dark happiness, she was relieved to be free of his abusive treatment. Yet none of his children could dispute the fact that Edward's legacy to them was his love of knowledge, which would sustain them throughout their lives.

Edward objected to the election of Woodrow Wilson, who was not only a Democrat, but also a scholar. He maintained that intellectuals were unqualified for public office because they lived in a world of their own. However, in his capacity as a country lawyer he spent more time reading Greek than in the practice of law. He defended women's suffrage, but he prayed that he would not live to see his wife cast her ballot. He insisted that he was a Republican on moral rather than political grounds, but he admitted that he would do anything to support the party's platform. On Mary's ninth birthday, in the election year of 1896, he posted a declaration that summarized those exalted tenets: "The Republican Party stands for honest money and for the limitless opportunity of every man to earn it." His daughter wondered, somewhat wistfully, how this noble sentiment had any relationship to her birthday.

Edward's incongruities were also strongly evident in his merciless judgment of human character along with his merciful treatment of human beings. He was appointed by the Governor to the Board of Overseers of the Asylums for the Insane in Bangor and Augusta and the Maine State Prison in Thomaston. He was elected to these positions since the Governor had every reason to place his confidence in Edward's wisdom. But the Governor was unaware of Edward's tendency to be overly compassionate toward the insane and the lawbreakers. He considered that they were casualties of tragic circumstances and his pity for them was irrefutable. He was convinced that all they needed was a new environment.

One September evening when Mary was thirteen, her father arrived home accompanied by a stranger. Edward's broad smile revealed his excitement as he ushered a meek, middle-aged man into the house. Behind a closed door he informed his bewildered clan that their uninvited guest was an offender serving time in the Maine State Prison. He advised them to treat Mr. Staples as they would any other visitor. "I'm sure," he said, "that all he needs to acquire new hope and courage for the future is a few days in a home like ours. At my request he has been allowed this brief visit on parole."

It was a costly five day encounter. After a sum of money and other items were missing, Edward discovered that Staples had stolen his wife's egg money, his daughter Mary's weekly contribution to the Christian Endeavor Society, and his son's favorite whittling knife. He returned Staples posthaste to the correctional facility.

But this incident did not faze Edward. The Chase family was not surprised when Mrs. Cook came the following weekend. She was a petite, elderly woman with deep lines crisscrossing her face and piercing blue eyes. She fantasized that she was Betsy Ross sewing flags for General Washington. Her serene disposition was ruffled only once during her stay. While the Chases sat at the supper table somewhat apprehensively, their guest suddenly jumped from her chair and began to run around the room. She pointed to the white tablecloth, to Mildred's blue dress, and to young Edward's red sweater and exclaimed, "All must be sacrificed for the flag of the free." While the children ate their baked beans listlessly, they heard their guest singing "The Battle Hymn of the Republic."

Judge Chase was elated over the almost complete success of Mrs. Cook's visit. Not only had his new theories on the salutary effects of environment been proved, but his troubled soul had been assuaged. The third and final visitor was Mr. Higgins, a former history professor; a short, stocky man with sad eyes and an amazing command of language. Higgins arose early one morning and went to the barn. The judge found him, stark naked, sitting astride Edward's Morgan mare, whom he had hitched to either side of the entrance. In his right hand he held a long pitchfork, and he announced loudly that he was Caesar Augustus. As soon as Higgins was suitably dressed, Edward took him back to Bangor. Upon his return, he embraced his wife and presented her with a handsome gold brooch in a garnet setting as a peace offering.

There were varying opinions of Judge Chase. Some villagers resented his arrogant manner, others admired his courage. In 1905, while serving as trustee of the Maine State Mental Hospital, he affirmed his liberalism. Seven years previously the United States Congress had offered Widow's Island, the former site of a marine hospital, as a gift to the state. Seeing no viable use for the property, the legislature delayed action. Edward created a sensation when he proposed that the island be utilized as a summer retreat for the mentally ill.

His suggestion was met with a stunned silence. The legislators protested that if the inmates were allowed freedom, violence would ensue. But the judge insisted that there should be no cause for concern providing that the patients were carefully selected. A heckler in the audience asked if he would be willing to spend a summer there. "I can't," he answered. "I have a family to support. But if the space materializes, I'll send my children there every year."

The bill was passed. Six thousand dollars was allocated for improvements and in July 1905 the center opened its doors. Virginia Chase remembered vividly her visit there in 1907. She was five and her sister was ten when their father sent them as "summer hostages." The girls had not been told the reason for the trip, nor did they know why the others were there. They noticed that these people had strange ways and this aroused their curiosity. Virginia and Olive were delighted with the lack of conventionality; they were allowed to do things forbidden in Blue Hill. They strolled along the beaches, fished from the pier, plunged into the tepid water of the pool. In the afternoon they relaxed on the long veranda where the only motion was that of the rocking chairs, the only sound that of the bell buoy. Miss Gracie and Mrs. Ober, deaf mutes, would signal with their long, tapering fingers, and "Miss Longfellow," an aspiring poetess, would write her sonnets.

Many of the patients worshipped Edward for they had been told that he was their saviour. Whenever he visited the center, festive preparations were made days in advance. "Dear Judge," they would say, "the dear judge is coming." Miss Longfellow composed a verse to be read on his arrival; another patient knelt before him reverently. As he sat upon his throne, a garland around his neck and a wreath covering his bald spot, Miss Longfellow recited her poem. The judge listened intently and then delivered a short speech. "It was not at all like the orations for which he was well known," Virginia observed, "but a simple, quiet speech, without even a gesture." When their father left the island, they understood for the first time that "here, among these simple people who had forgotten all about dignity, who knew nothing about logic or argument, or even justice, [our] father for a little while at least had been able, like them, to find a sanctuary."

Until his final days the judge attended the Congregational Church, always timing the Sunday sermon and often censuring the minister when it was too long. Edward Chase died in March 1914, shortly after his fifty-third birthday. His illness was diagnosed as nephritis, a painful and degenerative kidney ailment. His children were at his bedside: the oldest, Mildred, was twenty-nine, Mary was twenty-seven, the youngest, Newton, not quite four. As Mable read aloud an account of the wounded and dying horses at Waterloo, her husband's eyes filled with tears. At dawn he died, leaving the wide and far reaches of that tormented but still fruitful land that had been his life.

CHAPTER THREE

Childhood
1887-1899
"Thursday's Child Has Far to Go"

Mary Ellen Chase's generation was the last to be born literally and exclusively by the hands of women. Babies were delivered at home, often in the same room where one or the other of their parents had been born. The common-sense childbirth practices and beliefs which were later confined to the remote countryside were bequeathed to Chase's era as inviolate and sacred rituals. The doctor played a minor role, if any, and the father was banished from the scene of action. The expectant mother was attended by three predominant figures. The first, a midwife, necessarily a mother, stood by the patient from the start of labor to the finish. She became her confidante, therapist, and advisor; her job was to ensure that the mother was in good spirits and that any complaints she had should be remedied. In her black dress and immaculate white apron, the midwife acted as mistress of ceremonies, lady-in-waiting, and head obstetrical nurse. She supervised the bathing of the infant and had to be calm and prepared for an unexpected crisis. She received no actual remuneration, but customarily was given a pair of black kid gloves, a symbol of elegance and dignity.

Superstitions abounded in those days. The midwife had to be certain that the mother-to-be attended no funerals unless completely unavoidable and that she never gazed upon the face of the deceased, for in the first instance this would result in a difficult birth, in the second her offspring would appear pale and anemic throughout his life. The midwife was expected to concede to the fulfillment of the patient's whims, whatever cravings she had for certain types of food. If her desires were not granted, her child would have a surly disposition, or he would be born with disfiguring blemishes.

The second aide, the nurse proper, who moved from house to house, was usually a product of long experience. Her well-appointed calendar was arranged to provide two weeks at four dollars a week on each case, at which time the mother would be out of bed and back at work. In more affluent homes the nurse stayed for as long as three weeks. This shrewd, capable and energetic nurturer wore a starched percale uniform and was comfortably situated in the household at least two hours before the doctor was summoned. The bed was ready, the roller towels were bound to the bedposts to assist labor, the cornmeal gruel was heating on the burner, and the baby's layette was airing in front of the kitchen stove.

The third attendant was a female relative, usually a sister, mother, or sister-in-law. She served as receptionist, answering the doorbell, responding to anxious queries from neighbors, and placating the distraught husband. When the doctor arrived, he found a house completely staffed with competent women which gave him confidence that all would go well. His presence was almost superfluous and his fees were low because of the three efficient overseers.

Not only was the mistress of ceremonies ready with her part perfectly rehearsed and her subordinates entirely prepared for the actual delivery, she also adhered to certain traditions shrouded in mystery and folklore. There was the ritual of binding the mother's thighs in the early stages of labor with woolen cloth, usually red flannel in Maine country districts. Another convention used in rural areas was quilling, a device employed to maintain postnatal contractions as an aid to removing the placenta. A hen's feather was placed in the mother's nostrils to induce violent sneezing as a means to induce contractions.

As soon as the newborn uttered his first cry, he was bundled into a basket and carried to the kitchen where a blazing fire was awaiting, regardless of the time of year. Here he was rubbed lavishly with hen's oil or warm goose grease. Then he was carefully and speedily washed with tepid water and pure soap. His umbilical cord was severed cautiously to secure a good shape and size. A common curative procedure was the placing of a warm raisin on top of the stump, which was then weighted with a silver quarter sewn in sterile white linen. The baby was tightly wrapped in a snug belly band of warm white flannel fastened with safety pins.

Except for his diaper, the rest of the clothing was delayed until after his first meal, which consisted of a teaspoon of molasses and warm water, sometimes seasoned with a drop of lard. He was then dressed in a long flannel shirt and swathed in a blanket. A long flannel petticoat followed, pinned above the shoulders and over this a long white dress or slip. To complete the outfit, the baby's tiny arms were forced into the sleeves of a crocheted sack and he was wrapped in the ample folds of some durable family shawl.

After he was dressed the baby was presented with an amulet or charm, sometimes a bit of scarlet yarn, to prevent fevers. When the new arrival had been scrutinized, washed and fed, he was carried to his mother's bed. Custom prescribed that mother and child be inseparable, to ensure bonding, for the first two days. Later the baby's cradle, which had been used by his parent or grandparent, was placed in some conspicuous corner. From its slats a hymnbook was suspended for multiple purposes: it served as an inexhaustible reading supply for the mother or caretaker as they rocked the bassinet, and it indicated that the child would grow in grace and strength.

When Mary Ellen Chase was born at the Blue Hill residence on February 24, 1887, a blustery Thursday morning, the neighborhood doctor charged five dollars for the delivery and one dollar and fifty cents for each of two post-natal visits. The new arrival was christened Minnie Ella after her paternal aunt, a name she grew to despise. She joined her eighteen month old sister Mildred, a quiet, even-tempered toddler who rarely caused any trouble. (Chase always believed, with envy, that Mildred was her father's favorite.) Judge Chase hoped that his second child would be a boy. Edith, born fourteen months after Mary, was the brightest of the three and the prettiest, with lovely gray eyes, a graceful manner and a cheerful disposition. With her wide-eyed innocence and plaintive qualities, Edith was adroit at avoiding punishment, even when deserved. Edward Everett, Jr., arrived three years later, and as the long-awaited son, he was destined in his father's fantasies for Bowdoin College and perhaps for a Republican presidency.

Chase and her siblings were always referred to as "the children" and regarded more as a kind of corporate mass than as individuals. Although vastly different in temperament, they were expected to behave uniformly. Chase sensed early on that her sisters disapproved of her. They complained that she neglected her household chores, was always retreating to the bathroom to read, made up false stories and "put on airs" to attract attention. She felt inadequate and unloved, especially by her father, whose approval she craved. Her early fears of failure stemmed from his high standards and her inability to meet them. Her father often told her that, since she displayed no signs of ambition, she could doubtless some day earn her living as a hairdresser.

The children's upbringing was typical of the era. They were strictly controlled and reprimanded for disobedience, for not performing their duties, and for lying, at which Mary was particularly adept. Punishment included isolation in their room, the denial of pleasure, and frequently a sound whipping from a slipper or whittled shingle. The children were constantly reminded that the smooth maintenance of their household depended upon consideration for one another, that selfishness was sinful, and that respect and affection from their parents was possible only through good behavior. They were admonished to revere their elders, to have impeccable manners, to attend church regularly, and to do their best at school.

Chores were part of the accepted routine and allotted to each child according to his ability. Chase, who loved animals, was assigned the task of driving Constancy, the family cow, to and from her pasture across Blue Hill village twice a day. She did this from April to November in all kinds of weather and was paid five dollars at the end of the seven month period. Other duties, which Chase performed reluctantly, were the feeding of Victoria, the family household's pig, feeding the horses, bedding the cow, sweeping the barn, carrying food to sick neighbors, splitting wood, gathering apples, shoveling snow, filling and cleaning kerosene lamps, drying dishes and dusting furniture.

Chase was forever grateful for one chore made necessary by the presence of five younger siblings. By nine o'clock on Saturday mornings and on week days during the long winter vacations, she was stationed at the baby's cradle. By rocking the bassinet she was able to keep the infant asleep for two or three hours while her mother worked in the kitchen. As she rocked the cradle with one hand, she held a book in the other. When Chase exhausted the family library supply, she borrowed from every house in town, from the Ladies' Social Library and from the few volumes loaned every week by the superintendent of the Sunday School. Chase claimed that she prepared for graduate school by that cradle. Between age eight and seventeen, she did half of all the reading of her life.

Being a member of a large family had its special rewards, notably that of built-in companionship. In the winter the Chase children coasted down the slopes of Grindle's Hill for hours with an exhilarating sense of freedom. When the cold weather turned the harbor into icy patches, they spent their time by the fire playing the popular game of "Authors." Chase's early exposure to famous authors and poets enhanced her love for literature. In 1892, when she was five, the household mourned the death of John Greenleaf Whittier. From the cards in "Authors" Chase recognized his bald head and bearded face. She held writers and poets in high esteem, for she considered them to be unlike ordinary people. At the turn of the century authorship was a rare and exalted profession, a "calling" rather than a vocation. These writers lived in a special world, one of charm, insight, genius and mystery.

In the winter of 1898 Chase made her first literary pilgrimage. This momentous occasion was a gift from her father to commemorate her eleventh birthday, and it was one of the high points in her life. The author she was to meet was Laura E. Richards, a native of Maine and composer of many popular juvenile books, among them *Captain January* and *Timothy's Quest*.

On that February day the weather was frigid and the snow was deep. On the long cold drive Chase placed folded newpapers across her chest beneath her heavy coat, a soapstone at her feet and a hot baked potato in each mittened hand. At the halfway village of Surry, where she and her father planned to arrive when the noon potatoes would be baked, they would replenish their supply. Her father was silent during the trip, and the stillness pleased Chase, for it gave her time to memorize portions of *Captain January* as she wondered how these words would sound coming from the mouth of their creator. The weekly county paper stated that in her talk Richards would read at length from her famous volume.

It was an evening that Chase never forgot. The legendary Richards, a stocky, white-haired, vivacious woman, wore a dress of black velvet, with silver buckled shoes upon her feet and around her neck a string of pearls which she fondled as she spoke. Much of what she said escaped Chase's memory since she was more intent upon the way the author looked and the details of her attire.

After Richards finished her speech and began reading excerpts from her book she pointed to Chase, seated in the front row, and asked her to sit beside her. "I always did like red-cheeked girls," she commented as she held Chase's trembling hand. The fact that she was sitting next to this luminary, and close enough to feel her plush black dress shimmering against her fingers, was so overwhelming that the girl was speechless and on the brink of tears. On the drive home the next day, she could not utter a word to her father. Her composure returned, however, when she related to her envious sisters every aspect of the encounter, emphasizing her special treatment as she had "gazed upon greatness."

Eighteen months later, on a sultry August day in 1899, Edward Chase accompanied his twelve-year-old daughter on another remarkable literary excursion that would have a lasting impression. Led by their trustworthy mares, Jenny and Ginger, they travelled by carriage through the Maine countryside. As they approached South Berwick in the southwestern part of the state, Judge Chase suggested casually that they call on Sarah Orne Jewett. The judge knew Jewett personally and wanted his child to experience a direct encounter with Maine's Dean of Letters. Mary had already become one of Jewett's faithful disciples through her early love for *The Country of the Pointed Firs*.

Mary recalled that Jewett, who was fond of horses, thought Jenny and Ginger a wonderful team as, indeed, they were. The elegant and dignified fifty-year old spinster had been so extolled by Chase's parents and teachers that the shy country girl was awestruck at the thought of coming face to face with her idol. As was true of Hazlitt in his description of his meeting with Coleridge in *My First Acquaintance with Poets*, the occasion was to young Mary a "romance," a realization of all her secret dreams. She remembered only two seemingly unrelated aspects: what Jewett wore and one of the many things she said during the enthralling half-hour visit. She remembered how kind and gracious her hostess was and how she looked: tall and stately with features many described as beautiful. She wore a lavender dress with long sleeves and a high waistline and carried a matching lace handkerchief. Jewett had a regal air as she descended the winding staircase of her white clapboard house to greet her guests waiting in the wide hall below, her violet gown skimming the top of each tread. She held her head high and her classical, well-bred countenance was striking.

Edward told Jewett that the state of Maine was very proud of her. The self-effacing author replied: "Nonsense. Just think what I owe to it." The judge responded that she had already paid that debt a thousand times over in *The Country of the Pointed Firs*. His daughter was spellbound as she heard Jewett utter her first words, but she managed to control herself as she recited timidly some lines from one of Jewett's verses, "By the Morning Boat."

Jewett spoke for a while about writing and then she turned to Mary and asked her a question invariably posed to a child: "And what do you mean to do when you grow up?" To the chagrin of her father who, because of his daughter's reticence about her secret hopes had never before been informed of her lofty and ardent desire, she answered, "I want to write books as you do." Jewett smiled, a radiant smile that transformed and softened her rather severe features. "I'm sure you will," she said. "And good books, too, all about Maine."

Chase was certain that Jewett saw nothing unusual about her and merely perceived her as an awkward and bashful country child. But Jewett's presence was so commanding that, after this extraordinary introduction into the world of letters, Chase fashioned her own manners after Jewett's, and all through her school and college career she kept a framed magazine snapshot of her idol on her desk. It was always her most prized possession.

CHAPTER FOUR

Education
1893-1907

Chase claimed that her mother was not only her first but also her best instructor. Mable possessed all the natural gifts which constitute a born teacher. Her experience in the field was brief, limited to two terms in a rural school and one further year teaching Latin. She married at eighteen, by the time she was twenty-two she had three children and five more at comfortable intervals. As the mother of a large brood, this gave her a considerable range for the application of her talents. She encouraged the children to compose plays and games based on stories they read, to learn fractions from cutting pies and apples, and measurements from the dimensions of the flower beds and woodpiles. When the first four Chases were pre-school age, she devised an ingenious scheme whereby they taught themselves to read. In the large, sunny kitchen stood an old secretary, a high and cumbersome chest with six drawers and two wide shelves. To keep the children out of her way and, at the same time, under close scrutiny, she elevated them to the top shelf of the desk. She placed a roller towel around the two children on the right and around the post, similarly securing the two on the left. There they sat contentedly for hours, engrossed in *Oliver Twist* or *The Swiss Family Robinson*.

At midday Mable took a rest from her chores. She sat in the red Boston rocker by the window and read to the youngsters who crouched nearby on little red stools. Into the cheerful kitchen marched a host of familiar characters: Fagin, Hansel and Gretel, Little Nell. Mable's lively rendition of these fictional figures transformed the cold, drab winter days into exciting adventures in faraway lands. She taught them that the reading of fine literature was not only the mark of an intelligent mind but one's greatest resource. Her wise tutelage reaped its rewards; her five daughters became educators and authors, Edward a prominent attorney and state representative, Newton headmaster of the prestigious Thatcher School. John, the only non-professional, managed a moderately successful variety store.

Chase had other teachers in her formative years, elderly ladies who were set apart from others in the village because of their mysterious past. These women had spent much of their lives at sea with their husbands. On her weekly visits around Blue Hill with her grandmother Eliza, Chase entered a realm of distant boundaries, a world of memories, of wider thinking, a kind of humorous tranquillity. Their tales fascinated the youngster; as she grew older and dreamed of authorship, she decided to write about them, of what they had taught her in their homes that faced the sea.

When Chase was six she entered the same school her grandfather and father had attended. She later noted that, compared with modern standards, her education was mediocre. The approach was didactic, allowing the student little chance of self-expression. The children adhered to an inflexible schedule: from nine to four they followed strict instructions without any deviation. Surprisingly, most of them loved school, which proved that their training, both at home and in the formal classroom atmosphere, was highly effective.

The school stood on a hill overlooking the town. It was an antiquated building with two large rooms, the lower school administered to children six to ten, the upper those from ten to fourteen. Each room was supervised by a weary teacher, the product of a normal school, overburdened with more than twenty recitations a day. She had a student load of fifty; her weekly salary was seven dollars. There was no time for her to assess the potential of any student, nor did she display personal interest in her charges. On the positive side, she imparted an intense pride in learning.

To fail to complete one's homework, to misspell a word, or to have an inadequate knowledge of geography, resulted in disciplinary measures. In Chase's seven years at the village school, she made two spelling errors: one on the day her sister Olive was born, the other following the arrival of her brother John. Her penalty was to copy each word in her notebook fifty times.

Textbooks changed as seldom as those who taught them. It was considered that as long as the books were intact, it would not be prudent to update them, for the allotted funds were inadequate. The same reader was used over a period of many years. Chase, a proficient reader, was promoted to the most advanced book and knew it by rote. She sampled everything from the *Inchcape Rock* and *Lord Ullin's Daughter* to *Thanatopsis*, *Washington's Inaugural Address*, and Shakespeare's trial scene. When she mastered her lessons thoroughly, she was permitted to audit the upper classes, thus facilitating her adjustment to the Academy experience.

When Chase was nine she began to record her daily activities in a diary that she hid in a hayloft. At ten she entered a Sunday School contest and won first prize for an imaginative essay on Solomon's Temple. She prayed for a pair of ice skates as a reward, but was disappointed when she received a copy of the Bible instead. In 1902 she was appointed editor of *The Spectator*, a publication which featured works by members of the freshman English class at Blue Hill-George Stevens Academy. During her high school and college years she began writing poetry and short fiction; the sestet, "To Spring," was printed in 1903 in *The Mountain Echo*, a periodical issued by Academy upperclassmen. In December of that year Chase wrote "A Maine Thanksgiving" for the same journal; it described the anticipation and excitement of the holiday and the traditional fare served in her household. In 1904 she was appointed Associate Editor of *The Mountain Echo*; her third piece, "Among the Maine Hills," appeared that spring. On her twentieth birthday she received a check for twenty-five dollars for an original competitive story, "Why I Would Not Marry My Husband Again."

"Fancies" was printed in January 1907 in *The Blue Book*, a University of Maine publication; it was the first work she signed Mary E. Chase, later changed to Mary Ellen because she thought it was more euphonious. The story expresses her love of nature and abounds with colorful description of an unforgettable sunset: "The purple and gold lights were gone but the violet and grey remained. Over in the west, beyond the range of pointed firs and scraggly pines, was a real City Beautiful . . . Its rose palace and tower, and minaret-all of grey cloud with the violet light over all, and here I will say that the violet light made every home a palace . . . "

"Footsteps" is a contemplative essay about a day with a "tint of spring in the air, a lavender-colored day, at whose close one is weary from the very joy of living . . . I sit in the shadow . . . and listen to the footsteps on the street below." Chase identifies each person by the measure of his tread: an elderly aristocrat by the taps from his cane, a school teacher by her rubber heels and heavy soles, an unruly student by his careless stride. In these early compositions, Chase displays keen powers of observation, a distinctive style, and a prevailing optimism.

Blue Hill Academy, founded in 1803 by Reverend Jonathan Fisher, was among the earliest and most outstanding New England educational facilities. Unlike the village school, the Academy was well-endowed, and its instructors were often exemplary, trained at secondary and college levels. Aside from history and English and an introductory chemistry course, Latin, Greek, and mathematics comprised the daily course of instruction.

Chase entered the Academy when she was thirteen and became associated with some of the best teachers she ever had. Nellie Douglass taught at both the grammar school and the

Academy; she was a tall, slender woman with graying hair and rosy cheeks. When Mrs. Douglass died in 1942, Chase wrote a tribute to her: "She knew how to inspire her students with respect for good, careful work and hatred for the slipshod and unworthy. She said that a thing worth doing is worth doing well. We respected her so deeply that we . . . did not dare to fail her in our manners, in our respect for older people and in our sense of what is decent and seemly in behavior . . . She exacted the best from us, because we were always conscious that she herself gave nothing but the best."

The one hundred students were required to study math for three years, and as an elective most of them chose Latin and Greek. Chase, who was skillful in both languages, was eager to augment what she had learned at home. Her bailiwick was the debating club, known as the Webster-Hayne Society. Debates were held every two weeks between opposing teams with two students on each side. Chase wrote her own arguments and memorized them, the rebuttal included spontaneous censuring of her rivals. When she received a note from her father commending her spirited denunciation of Napoleon as a "monster to civilization," she was astonished for he seldom praised her. This letter became one of her most treasured mementos.

CHAPTER FIVE

College and Early Teaching
1904-1907

Although Mary wanted to attend Brown University because her favorite teacher was on the faculty, her father overruled her. He insisted that she attend a state-subsidized college. A local university would be less costly; with five more children to educate, the family reserves could be severely depleted. He wanted Mildred and Mary to gain professional experience either before college or between their sophomore and junior years. He was certain that if they had any aptitudes in this area, three academic terms would be a fair trial period; if not, a college education would be a waste of time and money. He chose the University of Maine at Orono since he had a high regard for its staff. He was aware that the girls would be in the initial group of twenty-one female freshmen and the first to receive coeducational instruction.

The Maine colleges, with the exception of Bowdoin, which had always been heterogeneous and urbane, were provincial facilities, not for lack of culture, but because of the sturdy, rural character of the students. Maine was not a wealthy state, most of its residents lived in country towns or seacoast villages. During Chase's undergraduate years, 90 percent of the five hundred students at Orono were local products, the majority from rural areas.

In March 1904, at age seventeen, Chase entered the University of Maine. Her wardrobe, selected by her practical and versatile mother, consisted of one dark blue voile party dress accented in white and fashioned with a stylish scalloped shoulder, made of white organdy and beaded with black velvet.

She had a brown woolen dress with detachable collar for after-noons and Sundays, blue sailor suits for everyday wear, two cotton dresses and three tailored shirtwaist frocks, a new winter coat, two pairs of shoes, a rather extravagant supply of lingerie, and a flamboyant gym suit.

The coeds were required to complete a year of mathematics and English composition. Chase not only hated algebra and geometry, but was a failure at both; she flunked math for three consecutive years. She preferred the orderliness of Latin, and the class in Greek was the highpoint of her day. Only Chase and one other girl elected this course. Chase was exposed to the limitless wisdom of Homeric verse and the noble ideals of Plato's Perfect State. Under the guidance of a young, radical English instructor, her class took daring excursions into the modern literature of George Meredith and Thomas Hardy. Hardy was sharply criticized at the time for his lewd scenes in *Jude the Obscure.* This innovative professor was demoted in rank, for it was rumored that he was intoxicated on many weekends. The report was confirmed when he consistently failed to attend Monday morning classes.

In English composition, Chase wrote plays and poetry in the Whitmanesque style. In 1906 she began to submit verse and short stories for publication. Although her work was not accepted, these rejections did not lessen her enthusiasm for the craft. During her first two years at college, she gained a respect for knowledge and an awareness of certain objective values, not clearly defined, but nevertheless secure.

Chase began teaching when she was nineteen; it was her first attempt at independence, and she was supported by her father, who urged her to learn the "brass tacks of life." He maintained that it was the best discipline for the retention of knowledge and also fostered maturity. His daughter was sure that among the reasons she was sent away was her disgraceful record in mathematics as well as a somewhat chimerical romance with an upperclassman.

Edward Chase explored the Maine coast in search of the most demanding rural school that required a teacher for the spring term. He found a suitable position in an unappealing district school in South Brooksville, later known as Buck's Harbor, a small coastal hamlet twelve miles from Blue Hill. Most of the twenty families were large, with eight to ten children; it was a community of fishermen, traders, farmers and sailors. The nearest academy was in Blue Hill, but few students pursued their education beyond the elementary grades. There was one general store that housed the post office, two boarding houses, and one small Methodist church.

Buck's Harbor was the counterpart of many Maine coastal villages. Due to its remoteness, the roads were in poor condition, nearly impassable in winter. Automobiles were rare, local travel was by horseback, long-distance trips by coastal steamer. The inhabitants were products of their environment; since they were virtually untouched by any external influence, they viewed the new teacher with curiosity and suspicion. Her appearance and manners were more important than any intellectual assets she might have. Maine coast natives had a tendency to assume the worst until they were convinced that they were wrong.

On the cold and misty April morning when Edward left his daughter on the steps of the school, his parting words were brief. His farewell gift was a razor strop, and he advised her to use it when warranted. As Chase watched him drive away, she wondered if this heartless man ever demonstrated emotion. When she entered the school house, situated on a rocky ledge near the sea, the salt air and fog, driven by the east wind, preceded her into a drab classroom. Her twenty-eight pupils, ranging from five to seventeen years, were hostile and ill-tempered.

Her first morning was terrifying. The thought of twenty-eight scholars and twenty-seven classes daily was so frightening that when she read from the Sermon on the Mount she almost forgot to include the Lord's Prayer, a shocking omission in those days. Since the children had no interest in learning and resented the structured routine, behavioral problems were acute. Chase began her teaching career with an undignified display of passions she never knew she possessed. She knew only that she could not go home in defeat. She paced up and down the narrow aisles verbally lashing her students. This outburst, aided by the threat of the strop, silenced the unruly mass; after that she had few unpleasant incidents through eleven arduous weeks. This was a major triumph for the determined apprentice barely older than those she supervised.

With a maximum of ten minutes per class, Chase soon learned how to apportion the time efficiently. Since some combination of groups had to be made if any child was to learn anything at all, she conceived the idea of hearing five recitations in rapid succession while the others were solving arithmetic problems. By being in three places at once, the math and reading groups were completed by morning recess, leaving time for four geography classes before lunch. By two o'clock the pupils were ready for history; spelling closed the day for everyone except the harried teacher, who remained to correct papers.

Chase's salary was ten dollars a week, two dollars and fifty cents of which were allocated for lodgings. Besides instruction, she was responsible for tending a refractory stove on cold mornings, sweeping the floor, correcting innumerable papers, monitoring those who were detained for misconduct, and placating a host of unintelligent parents. With all these chores, Chase's own problems faded into the background. She grew to love the children; their sharp little faces glowed on Friday afternoons as she read *Treasure Island* or *The Little Lame Prince*, for these tales opened a new world to them.

During these busy but lonely weeks Chase craved companionship. She began to write long, lyrical letters to Grace Cooper, the niece of William Daniel Hurd, professor of agricultural science at the University of Maine. On April 20, 1906, she described her quarters at the home of Mr. and Mrs. Billings,

newlyweds who owned one of the boarding houses. Mrs. Billings
was an introspective woman who did not encourage friendship;
when she was not occupied with household chores, she knitted
baby blankets for a Portland firm. The food she served was plen-
tiful, but the menu never changed. The meat, potatoes, bread,
cheese and dessert served for breakfast were repeated at noon
and night in varying amounts. Chase drank from a blue glass
mug, took the first helping and then passed the platter to the
others. Conversation revolved around the poor road conditions,
the native codfish trade, or Mr. Billings' obsession with lurid
murder trials. The stories he recounted were hair-raising, but
Chase liked the couple; they were simple people, kind and good.

Her room in the front chamber was small, but pleasant,
papered in elaborate pink roses with trailing vines. Her bed had
a handmade log quilt, the pillow shams were white, embroi-
dered with red daisies. She had a washstand with an ample supply of fresh towels, a bureau with a handpainted celluloid toilet
set, and one or two chairs. She was intrigued by the solitary
painting which depicted a majestic landscape but had some
glaring inconsistencies. She wrote Grace: "This [picture] is
made up of an immense wall of rock wholly surrounded by
water. There is a three-masted schooner in the distance and the
air is entirely filled with birds of all descriptions. On the top of
this rock two men recline and shoot at the birds. One falls but
the other 500 or more do not seem in the least disconcerted,
but still circle around the rock. I have questioned both the
presence of the men on a sheer wall of rock, as well as the brav-
ery of the birds, and I hardly think bird-shooting, a schooner
running very smoothly, and a terrible storm go particularly well
together. It seems to me both the art and the details are to be
criticized."

On weekends Chase shopped in the local stores that sold
everything from fishermen's sweaters to Peters chocolates. She
wore a white apron over her dress, carried a Boston bag, and
acted very dignified. The villagers were cordial; although she

did not know them, she responded to them, as that was the custom. On the way home she watched the darkness descend over the water, the appearance of the first evening star. The area was so scenic that she thought the inhabitants should have "artistic souls, if beautiful environment can make them."

Chase's interactions with the country folk prompted her to write about the "home life and the heart life" of the undemonstrative, reserved Downeasters. She wrote Grace: "It seems to me a great calling to be able . . . to portray the lives of country people. One can learn so many lessons from them. The greatest one, I think, is simplicity. They are so absolutely unaffected and still they never show their real selves. It takes sickness or sorrow to know what they really are but it is worth the cost." In this letter she expressed her admiration for Jewett: "Sarah Orne Jewett is, I am very sure, one of the best New England writers of New England people. I have always loved her . . . if you never read 'Rose o' The River,' do it at once. I think that is a perfect picture of New England home life and country life. That sums up my ideals. I never wish for more."

Chase told Grace of the wonders of nature. She listened to the tree toads singing at twilight: "[They are] as you like to take them, happy or mournful. It makes a difference as to what mood you are in. I get so tired during the day that I sleep all night with my window open and get up promptly at six ready for breakfast and my work. 'My work' sounds so grand. Of course, we have to work anyway, living is work, but mine sounds so different to me someway . . . it makes you hardy—the idea of work anyway, rain or shine, well or ill."

On May 10th she wrote: "[My letters] must have a selfish tone for they are selfish, all about me and that's all . . . for . . . I have little to write about except my children and myself. I wish you might have seen me driving over Monday morning in the rain. I got up at 4 and started at 5 with my pony and luggage. I couldn't hold an umbrella and the rain just pelted. The roads were bad and the rain had made them worse and we wallowed along through six inch mud. My hat brim filled with rain and ran down my neck and I had to wink to keep my eyes from filling with water. I was disgusted at first and thought teaching certainly was trying and then the idea came to me and I repeated 'Sandalphon' and 'Crossing the Bar' and 'Annabel Lee' the rest of the way. . . . By the time I reached Buck's Harbor at ten minutes after eight, the sun was shining and I felt as happy as could be."

By May Chase's teaching load increased to thirty-four students. One of the new pupils, Jennie Jones, came from a needy, shiftless family who lived from hand to mouth and pilfered whatever they could not afford. The girl was dirty and unkempt, thin and pale; she wore a shabby red calico dress and carried a small cottolene pail. She approached Chase's desk and stared at her vacantly with large blue eyes. "Goin' to see if I like you better 'n my other teacher," she said, "I'm nine, but I hain't read nothin' but the Primer." When Chase finished reading she noticed that Jennie was crying in queer little gasps. She was moved to tears as she realized that "the child has got to live her life without really living a day."

Some months later Chase informed Grace: "My little foolish child has died, or will in a few hours. She is very ill with spotted fever. The family lives in absolute filth and I expect the other children will go also. . . . In a way I am glad. The child has nothing in her life and she could never have really *lived*, only existed. I think it is a blessing."

At the end of the term the school held closing exercises. Chase was proud of her scholars who participated without making any mistakes. She later claimed that her indoctrination in the district school was the most valuable experience of her life. On the late June afternoon when she gathered her belongings, locked the schoolhouse door, and harnessed her pony for the long ride home, she was so pleased with herself that she forgot to collect her wages from the First Selectman's office. When she arrived in Blue Hill emptyhanded, her father was furious;

he demanded that she return at once to Buck's Harbor. That same night Chase drove back through the woods with a check for $81.50 in her shoe and the rest in her purse. The forest was dim and she had to be prepared for highwaymen. Upon her safe return, Chase was forgiven. Her father regained his composure when she asked his permission to teach three more terms before resuming her college education.

Chase spent the summer with her family, painting outdoor furniture and nurturing sweet peas in the hopes of winning first prize for the earliest pods of the season. The excitement in the Chase household revolved around Butter Cup, their new cow whom Chase described as "an aristocratic and free-spirited creature." One July evening Chase and her brother John volunteered to take the cow two miles across town from the pasture to the stable. A mile from home the wandering bovine was nowhere to be seen. Chase wrote Grace: "I started to hunt for her and after stumbling and ripping the braid from my skirt, I got her and fastened the rope on her hones. While I was taking the bars down she got away and led me a merry chase all through someone's long grass. I caught her and struck her with the umbrella and she . . . knocked me flat into a ditch. She went through the village with me after her, and a man asked me if I 'took the Agricultural Course at college.'"

On September 10, 1906, Chase resumed teaching, this time in West Brooksville, an agreeable community on the Bagaduce River. The village was more prosperous than Buck's Harbor and the work was easier. The students were educationally ambitious; many planned to continue their studies at Blue Hill Academy or Castine High School. There were two levels in one building: the lower school had forty-one children from five to eleven, grades one to six; the upper administered to grades seven and eight. Chase taught and supervised the lower school at a salary of eleven dollars a week. At the beginning of the term the village was plagued by an outbreak of whooping cough that reached epidemic proportions. Many of the teachers, including Chase, contracted the illness. The school board voted to postpone classes until early October, but symptoms of the disease were prevalent throughout the winter.

During the fall term Chase lived with Mrs. Blodgett, an amiable woman who shared her lodger's love of literature. On blustery evenings they sat before a blazing fire, reading aloud chapters from Charles Dickens' books, which Blodgett balanced on her knees below her knitting. The landlady was an excellent cook and a bountiful provider. She packed Chase's overflowing lunch box with two thick pork or ham sandwiches, two hard-boiled eggs, apples, cookies, cakes and a molasses doughnut, since she considered the ordinary white doughnut harmful to the digestion. Chase associated Blodgett with large red apples and Dickens, mementoes of their happy times together.

The winter of 1906-07 was bitterly cold. As early as November Chase was breaking the ice in her pitcher to wash, then hurrying to school in a piercing wind. She wanted to arrive before the frost-bitten children so that she could light the fire in the airtight stove. Due to the severity of the weather, it was necessary to find lodgings closer to the school. In December she moved to the home of Mrs. Robert Tapley and her daughter Harriet. Mrs. Tapley, the widow of a highly respected sea captain, was in her late seventies; she reminded Chase of the elderly widows in Blue Hill who lived "in a larger, calmer sphere somewhere beyond or above the trivialities of every day existence." Harriet, a postal assistant and the church organist, was a selfless spinster who cared for the family animals, did all the housework, and ministered to the ill and bereaved, travelling about in a smelly old sleigh.

When the schools closed from January until the spring term, Chase stayed with her family at the Hotel Pendleton while her father attended court sessions in Augusta. A photograph taken shortly after her twentieth birthday revealed a serious young woman, her fair hair tied in an informal bun, reading glasses perched on the bridge of her nose, her shoulders slightly stooped as she pored over a book. She was dressed in a white, long-sleeved blouse and a tailored dark skirt. Despite her solemnity, she had a capacity for laughter, even when self-directed.

Upon her return in April, spring had arrived in West Brooksville. The grass was verdant, the frogs in the marsh sang all night and the sparrows all day. The sea, blue some days and on others gray, afforded a "strange sense of companionship." That summer Chase tutored four pupils, three in Greek and Latin and a foreign student in English. She resumed her studies at the University of Maine in September 1907.

The campus had changed in the two years of her absence. The freshman class had two hundred students, including twenty women. She lived off campus with Alice Farnsworth, member of the class of 1908. They had three rooms: a bedroom, a small dining alcove and a tiny kitchen with an oil stove they named "Vesuvius," for they never knew when it might erupt. The girls did all the housekeeping and cooking and had their noon meal at Mount Vernon House.

Chase elected all possible courses in English and history, the two subjects she planned to teach, and in the Classics which she considered to be the best foundation for an English instructor. Her advisor was Caroline Colvin, an Indianan, who trained at the University of Bloomington and was the only tenured female professor on the faculty. Chase thought that Colvin's brilliant intellect along with her consuming interest in her students was a rare combination.

Chase graduated from the University of Maine on June 9, 1909. On June 24 Jewett died. Chase remembered the shock and grief which followed, not only her own, but that of all Maine people who regarded Jewett as the Dean of Letters. A few months later Chase submitted her first piece to a widely circulated magazine. "His Place on the Eleven" was about a boy who did not make the football team. It was published in *The*

American Boy, a periodical written for Boy Scouts. When Chase saw her first byline, she thought she "was made." She shared the news with her father, her severest critic. She wrote him a hasty note from Wisconsin, where she was teaching: "I am so happy I cannot sit still long enough to more than tell you the news received this morning from *The American Boy* editor $17 for a story called 'His Place on the Eleven.' Will have magazine sent to you." After reading it, Edward urged her to do another. She replied: "I will, Father. If I have time, I will."

CHAPTER SIX

Chicago and the Midwest
1909-1912

After graduation Chase began to look for a teaching position, preferably away from home. Many of her friends applied
exclusively to local facilities, but she wanted a broader experience. To expedite the hiring process, she joined the Clark
Teachers' Agency in Chicago.

Chase pictured the midwest as a rather exotic region, with a
more liberal outlook than puritanical New England. In a
locked dresser drawer her mother hid two books forbidden to
her children: *What Young Women Should Know* and *If Christ
Should Come to Chicago*. Mable divulged the contents of the
first volume when the appropriate occasion arose, but Chase
had never seen the second except in furtive glances. She was
allowed to read it only because her mother thought it would
convince her to stay in Maine. On the cover of this odd paper-
back was a picture of Christ solemnly approaching the crowded
buildings of a gloomy metropolis. It listed in fiery language all
the dens of avarice that the city symbolized. Mable's chief
concern was that her daughter might choose to go there.

In August Chase received a letter from her college advisor,
Caroline Colvin, recommending that she go to Chicago for a
personal interview. On August 21, 1909, she boarded a Boston-
bound train; her father gave her one hundred dollars, curtly
admonishing her that, should she require further funds, he
would charge her six percent interest. This warning did not faze
her, but gave her an exhilarating sense of freedom, for she was
finally on her own.

Chase had never journeyed alone, had never seen a Pullman car or eaten a meal by herself. On the cross-country trip she arose at dawn and gazed out the window to glimpse the strange new land. The flat expanse of the countryside, the harvest already reaped, the corn stacked in golden lines upon the freshly mown fields, equalled the Berkshire hills in its splendor. It seemed that the world and all it encompassed suddenly belonged to her.

Based on Colvin's advice, Chase planned to stay in a safe place, the Moody Bible Institute on the city's north side. She was met at the station by a sullen representative who did not offer to carry her cumbersome suitcases. Chase found the residents to be haughty, self-righteous women dedicated to the saving of souls. Living conditions were deplorable; the rooms were tiny, there was never enough to eat, and at each meal the lodgers sang a hymn with the chorus: "O to be nothing, nothing!" Chase feared that the repetition of this refrain might result in her own annihilation.

As the jobless days progressed, Chase grew anxious about her future. She sought the advice of Mr. Clark, director of the agency. When she told him where she was living, he was appalled, for Moody had a shady reputation. He knew of an exceptional opportunity at a boarding school in Spring Green, Wisconsin. The directors needed a teacher who would be comfortable in a rural setting. With Chase's previous training and her Maine country background, he was sure that she would be an ideal candidate.

In 1887 the Hillside Home School was founded by two progressive educators, Ellen and Jane Lloyd-Jones. They followed in the tradition of John Dewey, who had ignited the "flame of the current revolution." The sisters respected the requirements of each student as the only sensible way of education and they concentrated on emotional growth, the need for social and physical activity and self-expression. Hillside's aim was to provide optimal instruction for both day students and boarders. Jennie and Nell were aware that the success of education lay in the teacher's character and aptitude. The greatest asset she could have was a consuming interest in her subject and the ability to convey her enthusiasm to her pupils.

In a lengthy interview Chase was asked about her parents' role in her education. The verbal exchange included a brief overview of Chase's college courses and her editorial work at Blue Hill Academy. The ladies did not even glance at Chase's letters of recommendation. They were impressed by her unassuming manner and willingness to please. They hired her immediately as history teacher and assistant in English.

Chase could not believe her good fortune. She wrote her family: "It would be hard to find a happier person than I am . . . The Lloyd-Jones are fine women. Jane is about 60 and Ellen 55. Both have snow white curly hair and black eyes. They are the 'Ella Stover' type of women. The school is among the hills . . . and the country is beautiful . . . I have my living, laundry and $400 . . . and what I like best about it is that it is so unconventional and free that there will be no need of new clothes."

Chase's extracurricular duties consisted of supervising athletic activities and recording the girls' chest expansion to ascertain the increase in lung capacity. She was housemother to eight girls, aged twelve to fifteen. Frequently she employed her inbred Yankee ingenuity. One of the children who had chronic ear infections awoke during many a night in pain. To alleviate the discomfort, Chase placed a raisin on a hat pin and heated it over an acetylene gas jet, with a cotton pad she placed it in the child's ear. Within moments the soreness subsided and the youngster drifted off to sleep.

Before she left home Chase asked her mother to save her letters so that she would not have to keep a journal. But when Mable sent her a diary for Christmas she promised that she would write in it every day. In January 1910 she began to record her daily experiences. Her New Year's resolution was to make the world brighter for those less fortunate than she and to honor the principles of St. Paul, those of love, charity and selflessness.

Chase told her father that she would write another story, but she did not have a minute to herself. Every time she sat down with pencil and paper someone interrupted her. That winter she sent "A Washington of the Maine Coast" to the *Christian Endeavor World*, a Boston-based magazine. The editor, Amos R. Wells, wrote her that he wanted to condense the first seven pages to half a page. "They have nothing to do with the story," he wrote Chase, "and I am sure they would prevent it from being read." She replied politely, telling Wells to proceed with the revisions for she did not want to jeopardize her future prospects with the magazine. She wrote her mother: "A small way to begin perhaps, but I'm coming along sometime—I probably shall not get more than $10 for this, if I get that." When the piece was published on April 10th, the editor sent her a check for seven dollars; although she expected more, she thought that perhaps it was worth only that much.

By mid-February Chase began to question her role at Hillside. She wrote her mother a realistic appraisal of the situation: "I have been agitating . . . about the school, my work, and coming back. . . . I know I am doing satisfactory work . . . but I am not sure I want to come back. The location is ideal, but it tends to become very self-centered. We are near no one bigger than ourselves—we make the community. We hear few fine lectures, we see few people outside our own horizon and I find the atmosphere tends to make one rather narrow in viewpoint. . . . I think seeing the same girls morning, noon and night is a drain . . . I have to be so careful that I show no favoritism, that my speech never gets into slang, that I never breathe a word as to school affairs, or as to gossip, then some of them have been very foolishly jealous as to being with me and that makes things uncomfortable. . . . I am held responsible for so many persons and people look up to me. I am not a guiding star . . . if I get a chance further west, I think I shall take it."

Chase complained about her lack of freedom. The other students were in bed by eight but her lively brood did not settle down until ten. "This is a most personal letter," she explained, "but I am not at all dissatisfied and I feel myself fortunate. . . . I have made mistakes, but I honestly feel that I have done well in my position, which is surely a difficult one among the girls." Chase was physically attracted to some of her students; she avoided relationships with men, for she did not trust them. Margaret Rhodes, a pretty, gray eyed youngster, often came to her room to be rocked to sleep. Chase admitted that she was "getting dangerously fond of that child." When Margaret left Hillside, Chase was desolate; she sat under a tree and wept for her lost companion.

She also had close ties with her colleagues. Chase shared confidences with Olive Payne in clandestine bedtime talks. Jennie and Nell decided not to rehire Payne; Chase was "sorry, but it is right that she should go home. I feel keenly that maybe it is as well for both of us." Subsequently, Chase formed an intimate, probably sexual, attachment to Miss DeForest. In her journal she noted: "We are going to sleep out on the hill, happen what may, we can no longer resist the temptation, made doubly strong by the moon."

After spring recess, Chase's position at the school became more tenuous. She asked her parents for their advice, stating that the directors told her she had done splendid work and wanted her to remain without a raise in salary. Meanwhile, the principal of the Frances Sheimer School for Girls in western Illinois offered her a job as chair of the English department with a salary of $600. Chase declined, for she felt that the major disadvantage was that the school was affiliated with the University of Chicago, which preferred its own graduates on the staff.

She shared these sentiments with her family: "I like it here, but the responsibility is hard. The aunts are old ladies and not so keen as they used to be. . . . The life in the home is nerve-racking, and in other ways, too, I think it might be better to change." She listed her options: to stay at Hillside for summer term and the following year or to accept another position. Her parents urged her to remain at Hillside.

Once she reached a decision, Chase began to relax. Her role at summer school included tutoring six youngsters, washing, ironing and mending their clothes, and doing all the housework. She met distinguished professors from the University of Chicago who came to deliver stimulating lectures. One of the highlights was her encounter with Zona Gale, a perceptive chronicler of small town life. *Friendship Village*, a collection of stories about the midwest, depicted the camaraderie among country folk in Wisconsin. In her journal Chase expressed her delight in meeting the author: "I count this day as a rare one, as we talked much together. She is a frail, spiritual woman with ideals in her eyes—one loves her easily."

The summer routine at Hillside was a welcome relief from the stress of the academic year. In the evening Chase recounted her favorite stories of Maine seafaring days. The children were so enthusiastic that she decided to write a book, a collection of New England sketches. But there was little time for writing; her days were occupied with teaching, typing, bookkeeping, and planning the calendar for the forthcoming semester. At a chapel service Chase gave a sermon, "A Recipe for Good Cheer." Her talk emphasized the importance of making the most of one's opportunities. "It surely is a beautiful thought and I long to live up to it so that my life may be all sunshine . . . Miss Nell says I have grown more broad. I hope so, for I know I was narrow when I came out."

August 23 marked the "Year Day" when Chase left for the midwest and "glamour slipped from me like an old garment! . . . What a year it has been, what a year! The cardinal flowers have come and the road sides are gay with goldenrod and although the summer is going, the fall is coming and nothing else matters after all . . . I am glad I came West and shall never be sorry for I have gained in every way."

In September Chase was assigned to seventh grade, teaching freshman English and senior history. Every day she reproved herself for not writing the proposed sketches. Although she felt that the spark of genius did not burn within her, the 1910 journal contains some of her finest writing: "I long for gray November days ending in glory when it is not too cold to walk on the hills and watch the sunset . . . I wish the poets had immortalized November in other ways than in melancholy strains and dirges. I, myself, if I could sing optimistic, happy, stirring songs, and elusive dreamy things to express all I feel—I love it beyond any other month—I wish I were home to see the gray sea and the gray rocks and the grayer sky."

A mystical reverence for the human mind began to pervade Chase's outlook. She read works by Ralph Waldo Emerson, Emily Dickinson, William Allen White and Oliver Goldsmith. In lonesome moments, she was uplifted by Emerson's faith; she embraced his beliefs in the latent goodness and dignity of the individual and his concept of the "over-soul." Emerson elucidated the potential of the human spirit, the innate nobility of man, the joys of nature and their sanctity. He expressed what was in her own mind as something nebulous, but surely felt, in this turbulent period of her life.

By the end of 1911 Chase knew she had to move on. On New Year's Day 1912, she sat alone in her dormitory room to write her father a candid letter: "What am I? What do I stand for? What am I doing for the world? Am I going forward?" She admitted that she was extreme in her thoughts and actions; everything was meaningful and all-consuming without moderation. Those whom she admired she loved passionately, those whom she disliked, she censured for their disingenuousness, "frivolity of disposition and manner, lack of discriminating intellect on their part." She conceded that she formed attachments impulsively, and when she discovered some flaw that displeased her, she abandoned the relationship. She was overly sensitive to criticism and especially vulnerable when she was ridiculed as being "awkward." She denied any accusations of vanity, "for the conceited man places a false estimate upon his abilities and I think I regard mine honestly. I do not regard my intellect as superior, but above average."

Chase felt that her only endowments were a "gift for conversation, a mediocre talent for writing, and a gift of making friends, especially with younger girls." She thought she possessed a "certain magnetism" that attracted others and she knew how to capitalize on her charm. But she was aware of her shortcomings and feared that she was more inclined to "muse" about her assets than to utilize them. What concerned her the most was her constant craving for acclaim.

In religious matters, Chase was troubled that she was "no longer orthodox." She believed in God, extolled Christ and, in times of stress, sensed a "holiness—a reverence which often is entirely absent. I do love the holy and the high. My religion must not slip away—it must be a part of me. Sometimes the lower part of my nature triumphs and my thoughts disturb me. I shun all impurity of thought as something instinctively beneath me—and I do not at that moment banish it."

Chase's aim was "to love and serve those about me—to be honest and upright—to do my work for work's sake and not for approbation, admiration and praise. . . . If it is for me, I want to marry, to be a mother, to be the life of my children. Until then I long to fill my place well." She described herself as "unadorned, simply myself. I hope I may live years—so that I may truly succeed in attaining my aim." She vowed that in 1912 she would strive for two things: "to be pure in thought and act, to make religion a daily part of my life."

Chase worked at Hillside for three years. It was her first attempt at independence and her first venture in cooperative living. She maintained that whatever vision or imagination she imparted to her students she owed to the Lloyd-Jones sisters. To them, teaching meant fun, friendship, drama, the true meaning of life. They left a lasting impression on the young teacher who would, in decades to come, leave her own indelible imprint on a generation of students.

CHAPTER SEVEN

Montana
1914-1918

In the summer of 1913, Chase went to Berlin to study German. Her instructor, Fraülein Francke, was a sadistic Prussian who derived pleasure from ridiculing her pupils. Chase was the only one in the group who finished the course; the others departed in defeat as their stern taskmaster watched victoriously.

The aftereffects of this unpleasant experience were costly, physically and emotionally. While abroad, Chase contracted a bronchial infection, but did not seek medical treatment. By the time she returned to her teaching post in Chicago, she had a persistent cough as well as a significant weight loss.

In February 1914, Chase was summoned to the bedside of her father, who was desperately ill with nephritis. The two weeks spent in Blue Hill were marked by raging blizzards that enclosed the old homestead and made death seem inexorable. Her father's passing was the first loss of someone very dear to her. He had been her mainstay, encouraging and supporting her in all endeavors; her fervent desire was that he might live to see her acclaimed as a successful author.

One day later, Edward's mother, Eliza, died at her daughter's home in Bethel. The end was a blessing for the eighty-six-year-old matriarch who could not have survived without her beloved son. When Chase returned to Chicago after this double blow, she was in deep despair. The future, which had once seemed so promising, now held little interest.

Edward's death deeply affected the family's finances. With four children at home, the youngest not quite four, Mable was in no position to seek employment. Her husband's sole provision was a number of real estate holdings received instead of cash for legal services. Life insurance salesmen had not begun to approach professional men in remote Maine villages to convince them of the possibility of death and its consequences. Edward, Jr., assumed charge of the estate and sold the land reserves to keep the family solvent.

After two months at home during the summer, spent chiefly in coughing, Chase sought the advice of the family physician. Dr. Littlefield diagnosed her illness as tuberculosis, an ailment that was often fatal in those days. He consulted several specialists and they agreed that Chase should move to a more salutary climate, the Rocky Mountain area of Montana. Bozeman was their preference because of its altitude and since they knew an excellent doctor there. Before Chase left, Littlefield advised her not to have any physical contact with others, to sterilize her eating utensils, and to boil her bedding, towels, napkins, and lingerie in a solution of baking soda and water. These precautionary measures protected others from contacting the disease, but they imposed on Chase an enforced isolation from the outside world.

Chase traveled by train for interminable hours through the barren, sun-baked midwest to the gray obscurity of Montana. She arrived in Bozeman in the late afternoon of August 22 in a blinding snowstorm. The sudden transformation from warm summer sunlight to the darkness of a midsummer blizzard was terrifying.

Bozeman was a small city of about seven thousand inhabitants, located in the fertile Gallatin River Valley surrounded by mountains. Chase, who had never seen an elevation higher than the Mt. Desert Hills, was uncertain whether she should be comforted or intimidated by them. Montana still had many open ranges; cattle grazed on the hills as in biblical days, seemingly belonging to God as there were no visible owners about. There was ample acreage for homesteading, automobiles were rare, ranchers drove across the valley in rigs to do their trading, and cowboys were everywhere.

To a coastal-bred girl accustomed to sea and fog, Montana mountain weather was baffling. Fair skies prevailed for months at a time, with days of high, clear sunshine and nights of gleaming stars. When a warm wind blew in from the Pacific mountain ranges, rain fell in torrents. Winter temperatures frequently dropped below zero. After weeks of unrelenting cold, the thermometer rose fifty degrees in the space of a few hours. By nightfall, the air was balmy and a soothing rain shower began to fall, accompanied by gentle chinook winds that calmed the mind as well as the body.

Chase could not adjust to the winter cold. The sharp, dry air descending from the hills in icy streams was frightening in its severity. Loneliness seemed to fall from the mountain ranges at sundown and fill the valley. As she lay in bed at night, listening to the roar of the river and watching the rime frost the window, she felt overwhelmed and helpless. But during her three years in Montana, the weather became a resource in itself. The influence of the elements played a major role in much of her writing.

Facing life alone was not easy. Chase was especially vulnerable after her father's death. She thought of Blue Hill, of her mother coping with the children, and she wished she could do more for her. For the first time in her life people began to assume relatively little importance. The fact that she was ill set her apart from their daily activities. This estrangement resulted not in a sense of deprivation, but in a liberating sense of freedom. Books became her outlet; she read for long, uninterrupted hours, refreshing her knowledge of Greek, Latin, and German, contemplating the works of Dostoevsky, Dante, and Plato. The great essayists—Lamb, Hazlitt, De Quincey—awakened her mind to the infinite beauty of a well-turned phrase. She memorized passages that inspired her and imitated her favorites: Hazlitt's vivid monosyllables, Pater's skill in participles, De Quincey's perfectly framed sentences. She was bewitched by words, by the excitement of prose, by the fact that ordinary expressions could be endowed with distinction.

At the local doctor's suggestion, Chase went to the country for several weeks. The Wilson ranch was high in the foothills, ten miles from town and three miles from the nearest neighbor. The house was modest, but comfortable, with a barn and tool-shed in the tiny courtyard. Mrs. Wilson was a silent woman with large, scrutinizing dark eyes, always staring into space. She never spoke unless it was absolutely necessary, and her only contributions to Chase's welfare were her offerings of fresh eggs and milk. Her daughter, who was also somewhat aloof, spent most of the time horseback riding in the meadow.

In the golden September days, Chase went to the open range where a small enclosure of iron fence posts marked the gravestone of an unknown Montana settler. This site retained the warmth of the sun from morning to late afternoon. Its ele-vated, slanting tombstone provided a haven where Chase could recline at the proper angle for comfort. Surrounding her were the mountains with their glorious hues that deepened as the day progressed. She read most of the morning, ate a wholesome lunch of hard-boiled eggs and chicken sandwiches, and drank milk from a small stone jar. Then she would take a short nap lying in the grass, the sun's rays warming her back. At night she slept outdoors on an army cot in the corral. The air was pure, the stars brilliant, and the silence descended from the hills until it enclosed everything and became united with sleep. As she lay perfectly still, she could feel the earth turn eastward and observe her steady progress through the stars.

This recuperative period changed the course of her life. In the winter of 1915 she began to write for two hours a day on a regular basis. She had ideas for numerous novels, but the aware-ness of her immaturity prompted her to write a story for chil-dren. The result was *His Birthday*, a slim volume of forty-five pages, described by some critics as "belles lettres." A highly imaginative tale of Jesus Christ's sixth birthday, it was published in April 1915 by Pilgrim Press and sold for fifty cents a copy.

When Chase received a check for $150 from the Boston

firm, she stood on the street longing to meet someone to share the good news. She had few friends in Montana; those she cared for the most were in faraway Maine. To celebrate the occasion, she sent her mother a telegram and consumed heaping portions of chocolate ice cream alone in a dreary coffee shop. This delicious snack became a tradition in times of literary triumph.

By the time the slow spring loosened the ice-covered streams in the canyon, strength began to return to Chase. She spent the summer of 1915 in a mountain camp at Cold Spring on the Gallatin River. The solitary life suited her; the days were long and hot, the nights clear and chilly. She rode horseback over winding trails and through the canyons, fascinated by the sights around her: the flowers by the rivulets, the lupines covering sandy slopes, the Indian paintbrush, part flame, part feather. She loved to watch the scorching June sun gleaming on miles of silver sagebrush, the outlines of the hills, thin and sharp in the distance.

Although Chase had regained much of her vigor, Dr. Littlefield insisted that she remain in Montana for at least another year. Her pleas to return east did not make the slightest impression on him. In late August she returned to Bozeman to seek a teaching position. Early in September she found it in the public school system. The superintendent, Mr. Cunningham, a lean, completely bald man, was skeptical of Chase's teaching ability, and he told her this in the gentlest possible manner. But, since her presence in his office coincided with the unexpected departure of an English instructor, Cunningham hired her. Her position would be instructor of seventh and eighth grade in departmental teaching at the Irving School. The monthly salary was eighty dollars, five dollars to be allocated to the Palmer Method of Penmanship. Chase's handwriting did not meet Montana standards, though she practiced it faithfully under the guidance of a patient tutor.

The principal of the Irving School was Leora Hapner, a

Bozeman native in her late thirties and a genius at school management. She was attractive, tall and thin, with an olive complexion and startling dark gray eyes; she was honest and energetic, kind and compassionate. She knew precisely how to command the attention of the rugged, strapping youths from the ranges and ranches. She encouraged discipline, when warranted, and would wield a wide leather strap across the knees of unruly boys as they sat calmly in a chair without complaint and even respected her for doing it.

At first Hapner was reluctant to hire Chase. In addition to her inexperience in this type of school system, Chase was unfamiliar with western children and their ways. She had been ill and could conceivably have a relapse. But the resourceful headmistress was willing to take the risk. She was impressed by Chase's sincerity and eagerness to learn. From the moment Chase walked into Hapner's office and met the rest of the staff, she had the comforting feeling that she was precisely where she belonged.

The work was hard and exacting. From eight-thirty until four, Chase taught six periods to classes of forty or fifty, English grammar in three, reading in the others. When she was not teaching she supervised sixty students aged thirteen to sixteen, most of whom merely tolerated the rigorous routine. Chase soon discovered that these children were different from those she had known in Maine and the midwest. Like their parents, pioneers in a new state, they were intensely physical, restless, and spirited. High pressure tactics were essential to maintain order in the classroom. The pupils considered English grammar a waste of time, reading only acceptable if the stories had plenty of action. Chase was convinced that her chief value as their teacher was her knowledge of the sea. She was in great demand when she recounted dramatic tales of shipwrecks and pirates, which she told them as a reward for good behavior.

Despite the odds, young Montanans made Chase's teaching distinctive and adventurous. They gave her a respect for life outside of books, for their ingenuity in dealing with difficult situations, for their vitality and courage. Their lack of knowledge was offset by an abounding love of life and an intrinsic kindness.

During her eighteen months at the Irving School, Chase became an accomplished equestrienne, mastered the art of mountain camping, and learned how to shoot a rifle. In her leisure time she began to write her second book, *The Girl from the Big Horn Country*. The 320-page novel, set in Wyoming, was published in 1916 and sold for $1.75 a copy. Like its sequel, *Virginia of Elk Creek Valley*, printed the following year, it went through several editions. Originally conceived as a series of short stories, *The Girl from the Big Horn Country* represents the author's first attempt at writing a sustained novel, replete with lively dialogue, credible characters, and graphic description. The books appeared in two illustrated volumes entitled *Stories by Mary Ellen Chase*. They were promoted as "popular copyright novels at moderate prices, A.L. Burt Company's popular copyright fiction, published by arrangement with Page Company, Boston, Massachusetts." Other titles in the series included *Bab-A Sub-Deb* by Mary Roberts Rinehart, *The Adventures of Sherlock Holmes* by Arthur Conan Doyle, *The Betrayal* by E. Phillips Oppenheim, and O. Henry's *Cabbages and Kings*. L.C. Page, the publisher of *Pollyanna* and several other commercial successes, told Chase that he would purchase both books outright for $150 without copyright, royalties, or subsidiary rights.

Chase dedicated *The Girl from the Big Horn Country* to "the memory of my father who, perhaps, knows, and is glad." It was a solid achievement for the fledgling author who depicted the rigid boarding school routine with an accuracy drawn from her own experience. The "Virginia" series was written for teenaged girls, for Chase was aware that the young craved westerns. They concern sixteen-year-old Virginia Hunter, the motherless daughter of a Wyoming rancher. In the first book, Virginia leaves the golden plains of Wyoming to enter a Vermont academy. In its sequel, *Virginia of Elk Creek Valley*, the plot is reversed when Virginia's classmates visit her at the western ranch during summer vacation.

During this time Chase wrote innumerable stories, two for *The Social Circle*, a St. Louis-based magazine for girls. "Chickens or a Baby?" (November 25, 1916) and "Christmas in Bear Canyon" (December 16, 1916) concern two altruistic young women who make a sacrificial gesture based on their own sense of integrity. In these tales, the author extols some noble quality: selflessness, faith, humility, humanitarianism. The outcome illustrates the joy that comes from purity of heart.

Chase's literary output in 1917 was impressive. "The Maker of the Record" appeared in the February issue of *Youth's World*, a tabloid for boys published by the American Baptist Publication in Philadelphia and reissued in "The Home" (*Christian Register* in May). "Captain Peters' Pasture" was the lead story in the September 15, 1917, issue of *The Wellspring*, a periodical for young people published by Pilgrim Press. This tale has all the hallmarks of a polished story: suspense, fully delineated characters, and subtle irony. Unity of action, time and place, and the colorful rural Maine setting lend distinction to this nearly perfect piece.

For *The Wellspring*, Chase wrote the gift series, a group of sketches emphasizing the Christian virtues of thoughtfulness, understanding, and good deeds. The compilation included "The Gift of After Christmas," "The Gift of Sympathy," "The Gift of Extra Manners," "The Gift of Earnestness," "That Most Dreadful Thing," and "A Finer Sense of Honor." That same year her collection of stories on Island Homes was printed over a period of several months in *The Christian World Endeavor*. The three installments, "Head Harbor Island," "Petit Manan Light," and "Crowley's Island," portrayed the remote lighthouse stations that Chase visited in college and provided the background for "How Four Girls 'Discovered' Maine."

The story was published in May 1917 in *Ladies Home Jour-*

nal, two months after Chase entered graduate school. She wrote from first-hand knowledge of the poverty, illiteracy, inbreeding, and degeneracy among the inhabitants of remote Maine islands. "Four Girls" revealed an impoverished area of Maine that was virtually unknown. Chase drew on her own experience with the Maine Seacoast Mission and the inspirational guidance of its leader, Rev. Alexander MacDonald. It was based on Chase's travels with the mission in August 1916 when she and three other dedicated volunteers sailed on MacDonald's sloop, *The Sunbeam.*

In 1906, discoveries were made on the coast of Maine. From the islands, six miles from the mainland, came tidings of need and loneliness and sorrow, of people who were unfortunate, desolate, often illiterate because of the relentless law of isolation. These shocking disclosures prompted the churches along the Maine shoreline to turn their attention seaward. That same year the Maine Seacoast Mission was founded; its purpose was to lend a helping hand to island dwellers by improving living conditions and furthering educational opportunities.

Captain MacDonald, a Bowdoin graduate and a theology student, was the perfect candidate for island work. In 1905, after holding various pastorates, he answered the call of those who go down to the sea in ships with the strength and vigor of his dynamic personality. He procured a small sloop, *The Hope,* and began to investigate the dangerous waters. He worked with the islanders, caring for their physical needs as well as for their souls. He taught them how to fertilize their soil with seaweed, how to raise nutritious winter vegetables, and advised them as to the seeds they should buy and the winter provisions they should store. He erected small chapels as centers of social activity and religious services.

When *The Hope* and its successor, *The Morning Star,* became inadequate for his travels, MacDonald asked for donations from the moneyed tourists who owned summer retreats in Maine. Mrs. John S. Kennedy, a New York philanthropist, had *The*

Sunbeam built for the intrepid captain. In August 1916, the ship steamed out of the harbor, bound for the eastern islands. She carried four eager, determined girls: two from New York, one from Boston, and Chase. They brought with them a violin, a folding organ, a small lap harp, a play written by Chase, books and magazines, food, medical supplies, and good cheer. Their aim was to travel to the various lighthouses and become acquainted with the children of Head Harbor and Crowley's Island, Nash Island, and Petit Manan Lights.

Head Harbor was a haven of enlightenment compared to Crowley's Island, though it was difficult to communicate with the twenty or thirty natives, for the persistent forces of loneliness had broken their spirits. However, by 1926, Crowley's Island was transformed; the houses were neater and a school had been established. The next few days were spent in visiting two of the seventy-three lighthouses that guide the ships. They were Nash Island and Petit Manan Lights; the first a thirty-three-foot light and the other a one-hundred-and-fourteen-foot shaft, the second highest edifice on the coast. The keeper of the lights on Nash Island was a keen, intelligent man with a congenial wife and seven children. There was no law providing education for the children since the keeper could not afford to hire his own teacher. Except for the state-funded teacher and their mothers, these children had no means of learning reading and writing skills.

Petit Manan Light presented the same sad problem. Three families resided on the tiny rocky inlet; among them were thirteen children, none with school privileges. Lighthouses signified something more than beacons to the four girls; it made them aware that a summer colony, with all its pleasures, was merely a small part of Maine's rockbound shores. Through the auspices of the Maine Seacoast Mission the coast of Maine was accorded a special place of honor.

II.

The Early Works

CHAPTER EIGHT

University of Minnesota
1917-1922

By the time Chase entered the University of Minnesota's graduate school in the fall of 1917, her writing career was well-launched. At thirty she was older than most of the applicants, but better qualified than many. She did not expect an acceptance for she thought that the eight-year hiatus in her studies might be detrimental. She was thrilled, however, when the Committee on Graduate Studies informed her that she had been approved, tuition free and with a $250 annual stipend. The following year she was appointed part-time instructor of freshman English.

During the next four years Chase wrote five stories of exceptional merit. The first three were parables that presented a moral and conveyed a message. The fourth and fifth, "The Waste of the Ointment" and "Upland Pastures," are among the finest in her literary output. They display an unusual sensitivity to people and an intense respect for the characters' inner lives. Chase fashioned herself after Jewett in her portrayal of rustic

values, authentic dialect and tender portraits of lonely spin-
sters. With the publication of these tales, Chase was soon recognized as a commanding new voice in the field of short fiction.

"A Return to Constancy" (*Harper's*, November 1917) is the
story of Cynthia Blair, a compliant teenager, and her puzzling
predicament. She is responsible for driving Constancy, the family cow, to and from her pasture. Her dilemma is how to tell her
parents that she is tired of chasing the elusive bovine who has
an irritating habit of hiding in the swamp and ripping her caretaker's clothes. On a visit to the State House with her judicial
father, Cynthia meets the governor's wife, who urges her not to
abandon the cow, for she had a similar job when she was
young. She reassures the girl that the daily treks to the field are
precious, they acquaint her with the joys of nature. The moral
of the story is that the relationship between an animal and a
child can be of priceless, though intangible, value.

Chase was paid $150 for this piece, which attracted
national attention. Mary C. Robinson, a teacher in Bangor,
wrote her that it was one of the most charming stories she had
ever read. Florella Lowry, an instructor of high school English,
commented, "One of the most wholesome and human stories I
have read. . . . Please write more. I am on the lookout for good
things." Samuel B. Love, the manager of Mutual Life Insurance
in New York, sent a memo to his employees: "This simple but
beautiful story reminds one of our business. We need 'A Return
to Constancy.' We have a terrible war, and recently a serious
epidemic. Some have lost heart, the briars are scratched and
torn, and we feel like asking to be relieved of the duty. There
must be 'A Return to Constancy.'"

Chase had no difficulty selling her next story to *Harper's* six
months later. After reading "Marigolds," Lee Foster Hartman,
the articles editor, wrote Chase, "We are rather pleased with
your story which we are accepting for publication. I am a little
curious to know whether this is anything approaching a first

effort on your part. In any case, I hope that you are going to do other stories and that you will let me see them for it is very likely that we should want some of them for *Harper's*."

In November 1919 *Harper's* printed Chase's third story, "Sure Dwellings," a socially significant tale of a man's return to the comfort and security of his roots. Lee Hartman expressed her delight in a letter on August 21, 1919: "It is a great pleasure to have a story from you again and so good a one. . . . I hope you will try us soon again and meet with equal success."

"The Waste of the Ointment" appeared in the July 1921 issue of *Pictorial Review*. Helen Walker, the fiction editor, was so impressed that she asked Chase to name her price. She was paid $300 for it, the amount she requested. In this tale of unusual perception and astute characterization, Chase presents an accurate picture of Dorset, a deteriorated Maine village, which had changed drastically from its former days of seafaring glory. The protagonists, Emily Hilton and Exeny Douglass, are drawn with compassion and insight. The themes of loss, resignation, and redemption heighten the impact of the narrative.

In 1920 Chase submitted "Upland Pastures" to the *Atlantic*. The magazine had been her pillar of fire since 1910, when she began to send stories there, all of which had been rejected. On March 5 she received a letter from a member of the editorial board: "Out of materials which to an old manuscript reader seemed at the outset rather unpromising, you have made a story of unusual workmanship and living characterization. We cannot answer for the popularity of a story of this kind. It has not the quality of hopeful drama for which readers care so extravagantly, but it is in its own way a work of art and we shall be very glad indeed to accept it."

Chase replied with deep gratitude that she was finally admitted to the ranks of the *Atlantic*: "It may be of interest to you to know that I am an instructor of English at the University of Minnesota. I am, however, first, last, and always a New Englander, having been born and reared in the state of

Maine. I should like very much to know when 'Upland Pastures' is scheduled for publication."

Two years elapsed before the piece was published; during that time Chase sent several letters to the editor, Ellery Sedgwick, inquiring why publication had been delayed. She informed him that she was eager for the story to appear because of her position at the University: "I am to be granted my Ph.D. this next June, but it is through my writing that I shall win my promotion if I win it. I have . . . no time for stories this year, as I am writing my dissertation and preparing for my examination. That means I shall have no story appear to my credit in any magazine unless 'Upland Pastures' is printed. You see, a story, and especially one in the *Atlantic* means more to me than a doctor's degree, and I want most awfully to have the story come out."

Chase's persistence paid off. The piece was printed in May 1922. In this issue she shared honors with Lucy Furman, whose series "The Quare Women" exerted a profound influence on the lives of Kentucky mountain schools, the Irish writer A.H. Singleton, and Bertrand Russell. These luminaries were highlighted in "The Contributor's Column," but Chase's introduction was brief: "Mary Ellen Chase is a member of the English Department at the University of Minnesota."

"Upland Pastures" explores the issues of isolation and rejection that befall a young Maine woman at the turn of the century. The success of this haunting tale enhanced Chase's reputation at the University and ensured capacity attendance in her classes. An increase in salary made it possible for her to bring her mother and three younger siblings to Minneapolis; she set them up in a comfortable home near her one-room boarding house lodgings. She enrolled ten-year-old Newton in the public school system; when she discovered that the older students ridiculed his country accent, she transferred him to a military academy. She was also able to fulfill her mother's desire to serve as housemother at the University of Maine. Chase's sisters, Virginia and Olive, shared in the Minnesota life: Virginia continued her studies at the

University, and Olive worked as a librarian in Minneapolis until she returned to Blue Hill to marry.

❡

Chase took her orals for the master's degree in May 1918. According to her sponsor, Joseph Warren Beach, they were the worst set of examinations ever passed in his tenure. For the frantic applicant, it was a costly occasion. She tore a new pair of stockings as she anxiously rubbed one ankle against the other, ripped a lace handkerchief, and ruined a new jacket by pulling on a button hole.

Beach, an impassioned, agitated man, was always racing through the halls as though he had forgotten something, and in the classroom he was never still. He tore slips of paper into bits, broke chalk into fragments, and habitually raked his fingers through his curly blond hair. His mind was as active as his body. He was invariably excited by some new concept which made him leap from his chair in an attempt to convey his enthusiasm to the students. His mental acumen combined with his demonstrative nature gave his teaching a fervor that astounded everyone.

Beach was relentless in his bluntness. When Chase received her Ph.D. in 1922 he told her confidentially that her mind had baffled him for four years; it was not brilliant, not profound, nor even discriminating. This withering remark caught Chase off guard on that triumphant occasion, but she was inclined to agree that there was some truth in it.

Chase decided to take four years instead of the customary two to complete her doctoral studies, for with the onset of World War I, many faculty members joined the service and instructors were in great demand. Her dissertation, "Thomas Hardy from Serial to Novel," was written in 1922, but was not issued until 1927. She was so eager to see it in print that she paid the University of Minnesota Press $1,500 to publish it. In this study, Chase was painstakingly thorough in the comparison of three of Hardy's novels. More than half of the text consists of plot summaries and lengthy quotations; the conclusions are valid and carefully documented. Beach and his colleagues praised its originality and, as a bonus, Chase was promoted to Assistant Professor of English, a position which she held for four years until her resignation in 1926.

For four years, two at Minneapolis and two at St. Paul, Chase taught night classes in University Extension Work. She did this partly to augment her income, mostly because it deepened her understanding of the craft. The classes were extremely popular, for in the 1920s a writing craze was sweeping the country. In a witty essay, "Mrs. Penlust on the Damascus Road" (*Atlantic*, October 1932), Chase recalls her trying, albeit humorous, experience with one of her protégés. Amanda Penlust was not unique in her passion for writing, she was simply more exasperating than her fellow students. Her fantasy was to see her name in print on the cover of a fashionable magazine. Periodicals displayed housewives like herself who earned $150 in a single evening by the stroke of the pen.

There were two types of students in the group. Some created stories with well-conceived plots but without literary merit, others knew how to write but had nothing to say. Penlust was a combination: she had nothing to offer, nor did she have the gift of expression. Despite her teacher's warning that she had no talent, she persisted in submitting at least three stories a week. "Bleeding Hearts," the story she sold to a seed catalog for $3.50, was the most inferior composition Chase had ever read. When she asked Penlust what prompted her to send fiction to a seed catalog, the haughty author responded, "I didn't think at all. The trouble with you is that you think too much. The seed catalog was part of the vision and like St. Paul I obeyed it."

In 1923 Chase joined the staff of the College of St. Catherine as instructor of advanced composition. She held this post until 1926 and returned to teach summer sessions between 1927 and 1929. She was an active participant in convent life, assisting in gardening and in decorating an altar in the chapel. As a staunch New England Protestant, Chase had an overriding compassion for the deprivation nuns must undergo, yet the experience afforded her limitless gifts, justifying her conviction that religion was natural and waiting to be discovered. This enriching period provided the inspiration for several notable compositions. Between 1926 and 1929 she wrote eight essays of superior calibre. Four appeared in the *Atlantic*, three in *Commonweal*, and one in the *North American Review*. In 1929 they were assembled in one volume, *The Golden Asse & Other Essays*. This compilation consists mainly of childhood memories and of Chase's impressions of convent life. In these works, she clarified the paradox of spiritual richness and spiritual poverty, not only in her life, but in the lives of the nuns. The interlude at St. Catherine's was the only time when she seriously considered conversion, but she felt that the Catholic doctrine afforded a narrow perspective on life.

¶

It was at the University of Minnesota that Chase began her speaking career. The account of her many years of teaching would be incomplete without recording some of the rewards and dissatisfactions of a lecturer simply because she thrilled so many audiences. She was a natural orator; she had a command of language, a dramatic flair and exuberance which made almost any topic fascinating. She covered many subjects, from the joy of cooking to the wisdom of the Bible. She found herself in all kinds of situations which added immeasurably to her notions about life in general and human beings in particular.

In those early lecturing days, Chase had the lively companionship of Marjorie Nicolson, a colleague in the English department. When requests arrived from various womens' clubs in Minneapolis, St. Paul, or adjacent cities, Nicolson and Chase decided who was more informed on the proposed topic to be worthy of the ten dollar honorarium. When high school commencement season came, they received a slightly higher compensation: thirty-five dollars was the maximum, but a bonus was often offered. They marched with graduating classes, they slept in all types of homes, ate all manner of food, and listened to piano duets and recitations by a bevy of assorted children. They counselled parents on the rearing of their offspring and advised children on their careers. They met local celebrities, inspected parks and cemeteries, admired babies and sometimes cared for them while their mothers prepared supper. Chase learned early on that the mere giving of a lecture was the least requirement expected of a speaker.

Aside from remuneration, Chase lectured because she liked to. The unknown fascinated her and train travel gave her a sense of glorious freedom. She liked settling in the coach, placing her hat in a paper bag, drinking an occasional soda in the club car, arranging her pillows to read at night. She relished the assurance that no one knew her, that no one could phone her, that she was distanced from myriads of annoying responsibilities. The impersonality of trains, the solitude of her small compartment, liberated her mind.

The greatest gift that cross-country travel afforded was the sudden sight of unfamiliar things and strange enchantments. Chase awoke early one morning in Iowa; the long, wide fields were ploughed, the soil was velvety. The rising sun sent a shaft of light over the land so that the soft hues assumed a sumptuous radiance. In Utah she observed a late afternoon snowstorm. The gray desert was covered with sagebrush and the snow gave the illusion of undulating waves. One winter day she went north from Sacramento in the most brilliant sunshine she had ever seen. Mt. Shasta, white with unbroken snow, ascended into the bluest of skies; occasionally a great blue heron appeared above the earth, the sun transforming its plumage into an aquamarine of light.

In his essay, "Conversation of Authors," Hazlitt cautions his readers that although an author is "bound to write, well or ill, wisely or foolishly, since it is his trade, he is not bound to talk."

A lecturer may be required to expound, but she is not obliged to view the parks, lakes, and public buildings of the town, to offer her opinions on current politics, to be entertained by the most affluent families, or to eat in public.

Chase described the typical travails in the day of a lecturer in "Confidences of a Lecturer" (*Commonweal*, May 26, 1933). She wrote the article on a bitter January night in a northern New England railroad depot. She was alone, having declined the station master's offer of warmth and shelter by his stove until the train arrived at 2 A.M. She wandered aimlessly about the musty little room, which smelled of heat, lunch boxes, and dust bins. Her assignment was to deliver an afternoon speech before a womens' club in a large metropolis. She arrived at noon after a tiring 200-mile trip and was met at the station by Mrs. Brown and Mrs. Schwartz. Instead of taking her to a hotel to rest, they conducted her on a tour through the city. She was given statistics on the size and cost of the local YWCA, visited the library, the church, the skating rink and was expected to express amazement, ask eager questions, compare the sights with others she had seen. At one o'clock they proceeded to the home of Mrs. Schwartz, where she was escorted to the guest room and informed that lunch would be served at once. After a tasteless meal, Chase was forced to listen to one of the children play the piano, she admired another's handicraft, and endeavored to settle a dispute between the host and his unruly son. At three the ladies were informed that the lecture would begin in thirty minutes. Immediately following, the entertainment committee ushered Chase into the dining room to partake of more refreshments.

Chase was convinced that eating was the major curse visited upon the lecturer. Repasts for afternoon speakers were especially taxing, for the one thing a lecturer does not want is to be served a large meal before talking. A lady in Ohio asked her what she charged for one lecture; Chase replied that the fee was $75 without a meal, $100 if she was fed. The woman responded in a heated reply that deprived Chase forever of the $75 and the keys to the city.

But there were compensations in the life of a lecturer: the joy of escape from the daily round, the excitement of purchasing a new toothbrush, of packing one's suitcase, and of calling a taxi to be paid for by someone else. There were uninterrupted hours for reading, the anticipation of discovery within books and without, time for gazing out the window, seeing the snow-covered prairies of Minnesota at twenty-six below zero, the friendly hills of New York white with fruit trees, a meadowlark on a post in Iowa chirping above the rhythm of the rumbling locomotive.

Sometimes these benefits came from the audience in unpredictable ways. When Chase spoke before a worldly group of women in an ornate club house, a sense of yearning overwhelmed her. She longed for the reality of her bare classroom, the familiar stacks in the library, the welcoming smiles of her students. She searched among the stylish hats and unblemished complexions for some fundamental sign upon which she could direct her opening words. She found her inspiration in the black-clad figure of a very old woman seated in the front row. This woman had a light upon her face that was lacking in all the others, and Chase was forever grateful to her for saving the day.

It was for these unforgettable moments that Chase packed her bags, endured aching feet and the memory of her own words, ate too many chicken patties, and returned home tired and dirty: "For I am among those who glory in a country which . . . holds within itself so many sure and certain glimpses of eternal life."

CHAPTER NINE

Smith College
Early Years: 1926-1934

Before she left Minnesota Chase completed *Mary Christmas*
and sent it to Macmillan in the spring of 1925. Although she
hoped to attract an adult audience, the firm considered it more
suitable for the young. Louise Seaman, editor of the juvenile
department, observed that the text was "a little bit more like
the sort of thing that one reads as a delightful essay in the
Atlantic than the sort of thing one would buy in a book, but I
am very hesitant to express this judgment. I am so fond of the
character that I am very eager to persuade both you and me
that she will soon find publication." She suggested that Chase
send the manuscript to Little Brown and the *Atlantic*; a different publisher would be "very friendly to Mary Christmas's character and country. I am very sorry that she cannot be on our list
and I congratulate you for putting her down so vividly."

On July 10 Chase wrote Ellery Sedgwick: "You may have
forgotten all about me, but I wrote 'Upland Pastures' for you
some years ago. I am sending you the manuscript of *Mary
Christmas*. I sent [her] to the Macmillan people, as they asked
to see her. I have thought that she might be acceptable, indeed,
relatively successful as a book, but perhaps she is not made for
that. . . . Will you be so good as to read her? I should want for
nothing more if you should like her well enough to recommend
her for the Press." Chase explained that Mary Christmas was
the "golden thread in the lives of most Maine children a quarter of a century ago, and this little study is in the nature of a
tribute. It is a study rather than a story, I think. Perhaps, other
New England states knew her. I know she was often in Boston.

She was a wonderful person; it does seem as though she ought to find a public, if not a large one at least a discriminating one."

Little Brown published the book in April 1926, designating it adult fiction. The story evolved from two distinct impressions of Chase's childhood: the villagers' mistrust of the Armenian Gypsies who roamed the countryside at the turn of the century, and the sad lack of saintlore in the lives of Protestant New England children. It is based on an actual character who introduced to Blue Hill and to the Chase family a knowledge of sainthood. This slight, sentimental tale revolves around Mary's visits to the Wescott family (the Chase family in disguise), the emotional growth of the children, and the gypsy's enduring influence on their lives. This vibrant character foreshadows the archetypal, biblical women who dominate Chase's later fiction; they are indomitable and timeless, intimate with ancient lore, and endowed with extraordinary vitality. In this book, Chase pleads for a deeper understanding of those whose hopes or misfortunes brought them, strangers and alone, to a new land.

In January 1926 Chase resigned from the faculty of the University of Minnesota after eight years. On February 26 the *Minnesota Daily* printed an article by Cecil Moore, professor of English and chairman of that department: "Miss Chase's resignation means to us . . . that we have lost one of our most gifted and stimulating teachers. It is not difficult to know what a high value her students place upon her work, and colleagues have been no less enthusiastic, and there is not one of them who will not regard her departure as a serious personal, as well as professional loss." Martin Ruud, associate professor of English, commented, "This is a matter about which it is difficult to say anything without divulging in superlatives. Her going will be an irreparable loss . . . she is undoubtedly one of the best, if not the best instructor in her line of work that we have ever had. She is a rare person, one who has a way of her own of inspiring her students, of carrying them along with her in her enthusiasm, and of making them appreciate all that is beautiful and fine in literature."

Marguerite Wells, a graduate of Smith in 1895, director of the Alumnae Association in 1917 and 1918, and a trustee from 1920 to 1930, attended many of Chase's lectures and was impressed with her dynamic delivery. She wrote President Neilson suggesting that he enlist Chase to serve on the Smith faculty. He wrote her in January 1926, proposing an associate professorship in English language and literature commencing the following September; he added that there would be a definite opportunity for advancement. Most universities did not advocate promotion of females; the womens' colleges raised no such barrier.

Chase's annual salary at Minnesota was $2,800; Neilson offered $3,000: "I am making this offer without having a chance to find out in detail about your present rank and salary, but I am hoping that you will write me frankly about any aspect of the proposal that you want to discuss." Chase replied that her only request was that she be granted sufficient time for writing. Neilson promised that she could devote two days a week toward this endeavor.

Smith College appealed to Chase because of its manageable size, the quality of the faculty, and the outstanding calibre of its leader. Neilson was famous for his acerbic wit as well as for his scholarly credentials, and the girls revered him. Chase admired his interpretation of English poetry, had read his books and had heard him speak to captive audiences. He was not only a great teacher, but one who cared for his faculty. He expected them to express their individual opinions, to be honest with their students, and to respect past wisdom.

Early in her career at Smith, Chase told Neilson that she had no time to accept dinner invitations from students. He remarked: "Now I could let you off from teaching . . . or from reading your themes, but I really couldn't let you off from tea or dinner. Perhaps you don't know it yet, but to go to tea and dinner with freshmen happens to be the most important thing you're doing around this place . . . Remember that a teacher who isn't asked to tea and dinner probably isn't worth her salt, and don't come asking again to be let off from what is your most important job in this college."

When Chase came to Smith she rented a dreary flat in downtown Northampton with Margaret Eliot Macgregor, close friend and colleague at the University of Minnesota. Two years later Chase was promoted to full professor. Rapid advancement was customary, for there were many opportunities for upward mobility. In her three decades at Smith Chase was recognized as one of the stellar figures in the annals of the college. She had a contagious enthusiasm, a capacity for conveying a love not only for literature, but for life itself.

Macgregor was another rising star on campus. In her four years there she was esteemed as an exceptional instructor who combined a knowledge of her subject with a keen perception of each individual's needs. In 1930 Macgregor was appointed Dean of the class of 1936, a position she was to assume in February 1933. An earlier desire to go abroad for further research was more clearly defined at Smith. She was granted a two-year leave of absence to pursue a Ph.D. degree at the University of London, which she received in June 1932.

The year Macgregor spent in England was a period of intense physical pain as she battled courageously against the illness which finally claimed her. Macgregor never returned to Smith; she died of a brain tumor in October 1932 at her Missouri home. Chase was heartbroken.

At that time it was not unusual for women to set up house-keeping together, to share work and friendship, to strive toward a common goal. These female attachments were regarded as standard practice, not always linked to sexual preference. But, in Chase's case, there were obvious carnal overtones. In *The Bostonians* (1886), Henry James wrote about the relationship between Olive Chancellor and Verena Tarrant, a study of one of those friendships between women which were common in New England, known as a "Boston marriage." In her journal Margaret Fuller reflected on her alliance with Anna Barker: "It is so true that a woman may be in love with a woman and a man with a man . . . It is regulated by the same law as that of love between persons of different sexes, only it is purely intellectual and spiritual, unprofaned by any mixture of lower interests."

Chase's role model, Sarah Orne Jewett, formed such a union with Annie Fields shortly after James Fields' death. The Jewett-Fields ménage was an example of two women living harmoniously in a matrimonial-like bond, a physical closeness which Jewett described as "all as natural as can be." Willa Cather also had intense feelings for women. In 1903 she met Edith Lewis, a Smith alumna, and five years later they established living quarters in New York. After Cather's death in 1947 Lewis retained her love for the "genius she had discovered" until her own death in 1972. Their interment next to each other in East Jaffrey, New Hampshire, indicates the extent of their devotion.

Shortly after Macgregor's death, Chase found another roommate: Eleanor Shipley Duckett, professor of Classical Languages and Literature. At first, both women had reservations about living together—Duckett because she felt better suited to a solitary existence, Chase because she feared that no one could replace Macgregor. "I have Eleanor living with me," she wrote Mildred Hillhouse, a Minnesota friend. "She is awfully nice, but not Margaret." Thus Chase embarked rather dubiously upon a relationship that would become legendary in the annals of the college and would endure for more than forty years.

Chase and Duckett met in October 1928 in the college library, where both were writing books in adjacent carrels. Suddenly, Duckett became aware of a "vibrating energy" radiating nearby. She hesitated for a moment, trying to locate the source of this disturbance. She soon discovered Chase writing furiously at the next table, "with a bubbling rapture of concen-

tration so eager that the air seemed to swirl with activity."
Looking up, Duckett noticed a bevy of students flocking around
Chase's desk, hoping to receive a glimmer of recognition or a
hasty word of advice. Her curiosity sufficiently aroused,
Duckett asked a friend to introduce her to this human energy
field. Immediately, the women were attracted to each other. In
1934 they moved to 16 Paradise Road, a tidy white clapboard
house next to the president's stately residence.

Although born and raised on opposite continents in vastly
different circumstances, Chase and Duckett shared a common
kinship, the bond of blood that unites old Maine families to
the English race. But it was more than this that allied them.
Both had been dominated by controlling fathers intent on their
academic success. Both were dedicated to the role of spinster-
hood and considered their work more important than marriage.
Neither felt the two could be combined successfully. They
chose not to wed, not did they wish for the chance to choose,
for they found a refreshing liberation in their freedom. They
devoted their lives to study, research, and writing, and they
established reputations as lively teachers, thoroughly grounded
in their fields. They had the scholar's virtues of patience, dili-
gence, and integrity and a fine sensitivity to the English language.

Like Cather and Lewis, Chase and Duckett were close professional colleagues as well as loyal friends. Chase craved fame
and admiration, though she was reluctant to admit it. Duckett,
proud of her mate's renown, maintained a low profile, often
acting as buffer between Chase and the demands of the outside
world. Discerning associates observed that Chase was the dominant partner, the nurturer and caregiver who planned the
meals, ironed and mended Duckett's clothes, and usually
selected her wardrobe. Chase disapproved of Duckett's preference for masculine attire and urged her to dress in a more lady-
like fashion. She possessed the skills that Duckett lacked and
encouraged her to be more sociable; every other week they

dined with friends in a local restaurant, always ordering the same meal.

Their association was genuine and enduring. Their personalities, although dissimilar, complemented one another. Chase was a forceful person with great charisma, outwardly self-assured, and a meticulous housekeeper. Duckett was quiet, withdrawn and reticent, not at all interested in domestic affairs. She seldom made excessive demands on Chase; she provided love and support without being intrusive. On their frequent trips to England they reserved separate cabins and adjoining rooms in hotels. Any conflict that arose between them was the result of Chase's condescending manner toward her "helpless" friend and Duckett's concern regarding this attitude. Duckett felt that she was not nearly so absent-minded or involved with her saints as Chase perceived her to be. "Living with a mystic has its limitations," Chase wrote a friend, "the world she lives in is just the right one for her, although it would never do for me."

Duckett's daily absence in the library to pursue research afforded Chase time to read, to meditate, and to be alone. Chase, who was more creative than cerebral, needed to be enrooted in a familiar space in which to write. Her favorite area was at the dining room table. She scribbled her fiction on yellow legal pads purchased at the five and dime; she placed a brown paper bag on the hardwood surface to prevent marring. A silver vase of fresh flowers faced her and her white hair was wrapped in tissue so that the cigarette smoke would not discolor it. When Duckett arrived home for lunch her friend surprised her with an appetizing salad, a special iced beverage, or a dish of artichokes. As they relaxed over the meal, they reviewed the happenings of the day.

Although Duckett was surrounded by her books, she was not isolated by them. She made significant contributions to Smith's development program and played a primary role in extracurricular affairs. She had a loyal and considerable following; a campus favorite, at academic processions the sight of her petite, red-robed figure drew a hearty round of applause.

Chase felt incomplete without "wonderful, generous Eleanor." She could not have achieved her prolific literary output without the support and encouragement of her friend who always proofread her fiction. They were so close that Chase feared that Duckett might become ill or meet with some sudden mishap. In her journal she wrote: "I adore [Eleanor], her lovely mind, her fumbling hands, her omnipresent eagerness and joy. . . . She has been sweetness itself, helpful, inimitable and lovely." Their intertwined lives were a "harmony of all things human and divine," they gave each other "mysterious moments of faith, hope and fun." There was something solid, yet intangible, between them that had little to do with similarity of taste or sameness in training. They were companions of the heart, whether together or apart they found each other "terribly exciting" and loved one another "beyond words." To demonstrate their mutual affection, Duckett once said: "We kneel Sunday after Sunday in St. John's Church, I in the pew in front of her, she in the one directly behind. We like to be a little alone; but at the altar she sometimes tucks her hand in mine."

In *Writing A Woman's Life* (W.W. Norton, 1988) Carolyn Heilbrun observed that "we have learned to guess how often in the past, their stories only now emerging, women in the public sphere have loved other women, and drawn from that love what men draw not from the companionship of other men but from the friendship and support of women. We begin to surmise that if we look beyond the public face of those few notable women in the past . . . we may find an untold story of friendship between women, sustaining but secret."

Heilbrun cited the strong attachment between Vera Brittain and Winifred Holtby, who met at Somerville College in Oxford, England, after World War I. Their friendship ended in 1917 when Holtby died of kidney disease. Only death could sever their alliance, "neither marriage, nor distance, nor illness would have done so." For these women friendship signified the enabling bond that not only "supported risk and danger but also comprehended the details of a public life and the complexities of pain found there."

In the prologue to *Testament of Friendship* (1940) Brittain remarked that the friendships of women "have usually been not merely unsung, but mocked, belittled and falsely interpreted." When she wrote of her bond with Holtby, she felt that she had to protect herself from accusations of homosexuality: "To deny those feminine individualists who believe they flatter men by fostering the fiction of women's jealous ability to love and respect each other was easy enough." She felt impelled to answer those "other skeptics who are roused by any record of affection between women to suspicions habitual among the over-sophisticated." After Brittain's marriage, Holtby encouraged her to struggle "against the tradition that domesticity must be the first concern of wife and mother." Heilbrun maintained that "the sign of female friendship is not whether friends are homosexual or heterosexual, lovers or not, but whether they share the wonderful energy of work in the public sphere." For Chase, friendship meant both physical pleasure and intellectual gratification.

¶

In 1927 Chase wrote *Uplands*, a melancholy love story set in the fictional village of North Dorset, Maine, "a partly real, partly dream country." It was based on her piece, "The Garment of Praise," which appeared in *Scribner's* (October 1925). In the preface she implies that the tale is neither a tragedy nor a comedy, but a romance. The emphasis is on the elegaic quality of the land and its effect on the inhabitants. The coast dwellers are victims of the harsh environment that ultimately seals their fate. The characters have little control over their lives; they merely endure and are resigned to their lot. The author's ability to depict simple life on her own turf gives this novel its singular qualities.

Between 1928 and 1934 Chase wrote several short stories, a book of essays (*The Golden Asse*), a textbook for college freshmen (*The Writing of Informal Essays*, 1928) and *A Goodly Heritage* (1932). In 1930 she composed a book for children, *The Silver Shell*, based on her teaching experience with the Maine Seacoast Mission. Her most notable achievement that year was the story "Salesmanship," published in the July issue of *Pictorial Review*. Selected from 11,000 applicants, she was awarded first prize of $2,500. With the money Chase bought a blue whirl eggbeater, the best and sharpest axe for $3.50, and half a cord of unsplit wood. In September she purchased a new Ford and sold it at a loss two weeks later. During that time she collided with two cherry trees, a lawnmower, a Plymouth Rock rooster, an empty baby carriage, and a speeding Packard.

Chase admitted that she was a terrible driver. The engine meant nothing to her, nor could she understand the manual. This experience made her poorer but wiser. She was grateful to be alive, for she would not have been had she kept the Ford. On June 13 she sailed on the *Homeric* to spend time alone in Cornwall. She would remain there until "my neck stops aching and my stomach is again normal."

CHAPTER TEN

The Maine Novels
1934-1935

Mary Peters, 1934

When Chase was growing up at the turn of the century, she was aware of the transformation brought about by the Industrial Revolution. Barques and clipper ships were replaced by coastwise steamers and speed boats; as Maine's maritime power declined, the natives were caught in the vise of change. The peace and security they had once known was destroyed by the free-spending tourists. The villages no longer belonged to their rightful owners: "By 1905 change had settled itself into comparative stability . . . shipbuilding was over, and Maine had given itself up to the necessities of the alien population which afforded its sustenance during the summer and excused its idleness during the winter."

This was the Maine that Chase knew, a state at the crossroads between the old and the new, between the great seafaring days when "foreign ports were household words" and the era of evolution wrought by the invasion of wealthy vacationers. Rich men bought headlands and paid outrageous prices for their homes. They built golf courses, purchased heirlooms, and created a market for hooked rugs. The courageous old sea captains who had previously commanded respect became objects of scorn and derision.

When Chase began to write about Maine people and places, Sarah Orne Jewett was her model. She was profoundly influenced by Jewett's novel, *Deephaven*, a series of sketches of a once prosperous seaport whose commerce had vanished and whose harbor was filled with debris. Although three decades separated them, Chase and Jewett grew up in a period of industrial change. They saw the decline of New England as rich material for fiction and they "sentimentally, moralistically, and realistically chronicled this decline." They confirmed the positive values of Downeasters, the hardy, deep-rooted parts which formed the New England character at its best, thus preserving vital records of the people, conditions, and values of nineteenth-century rural New England. Chase's objective was to perpetuate the spirit of a splendid past and extol the virtues which endured. The most valuable elements in her work stem from her sure knowledge of the circumscribed life she had known. She discovered in the demise of a region not only a meaningful relationship to twentieth-century realities, but the source of a country's strength and ongoing spiritual heritage. Chase carried the chronicle forward, elevating the regional novel to its highest level by paying homage to the past.

Mary Peters was conceived in Chase's mind twenty-five years before the fictional village of Petersport had any shape at all. Its beginnings reach back to her childhood when her grandmother Eliza recounted tales about life at sea. Eliza imparted an understanding of the gifts as well as the terrors of the sea, the sense of a greater world beyond the small harbors and Maine hills.

Although the heroine is named for Chase's great-great-grandmother, she maintained that no character is ever based on an actual person, but is a composite of many. She claimed that a novel is a "portrayal of life as it actually was lived and its aim is truth." Mary Peters is based securely on Maine history and life. As the story moves into a metaphysical probing of man's existence, it never leaves the world of precise detail. It is replete with the roster of crews, ports, weather, and animals to the minutiae of dress, morals, manners, and education. Her portrayal of life in the 1880s was created to show how a childhood spent largely at sea "might help to form a mind and an imagination invulnerable against time, chance, and tragedy."

The narrative revolves around the adventures of Mary Peters, who was born on her father's ship and remained aboard for fifteen years. When she was fifteen, the ship arrived in San Francisco; Mary and her mother, Sarah, debarked to return to Petersport, where Mary would attend the Academy. While they slept peacefully in a local hotel, the ship was hurled down the coast in a savage storm and dashed against a reef. The crew perished, along with Mary's father and her beloved teacher, Mr. Gardiner.

When Mary and her mother arrived in Petersport, they noticed a dramatic change in the village. The docks were deserted, its piers rotting. The war had taken its toll of men and ships and made ocean traffic precarious; iron and steel were used instead of wood to build ships and coastal steamers were increasing in number. Sarah mourned the transformation that was engulfing the coast: "There was something in the sight of a grandson of a shipmaster in the foreign trade, shingling the roof of a summer cottage for his livelihood . . . there was something sadder in the knowledge that strangers . . . knew little and cared less for the boy's history."

As an observer, Chase was able to judge Maine character objectively. She recognized the flaws that made Downeasters vulnerable to easy money on the coast. She detected a certain shrewdness in their outlook, acquired through more than two centuries of struggle. The villagers often surrendered to temptation; their materialistic desires resulted in the loss of integrity. Academy graduates abandoned plans for further education; instead, they became maids and gardeners of the rich and caddies on golf links. Fishermen discarded their nets to serve as tourist guides, and local merchants raised their prices to ensure a profit. A sympathetic visitor commented on the cruel indifference of the interloper: "It must be hard for you to see strangers in your old houses, to have your village overrun by outsiders . . . I don't suppose people who come here . . . know very much about the history of a place like this even though they take up residence here to escape city taxes. Perhaps they don't even care much."

The invasion of the coast marked a change as extensive as it was inevitable. The natives' greediness belittled them in the eyes of their employers; their hopes of emulating their rich masters resulted in bitterness and frustration. "It would be helpful all around," one of the characters observed, "and save a lot of misunderstanding if [the outsider] knew a bit about the best of us."

In Chase's fiction, man is not always the master of his fate. When he encounters adversity, he may succumb and submit, or he may assess the struggle as ineluctable. If one cannot overcome the assaults of fate, he can survive with dignity by drawing strength from the deepest sources of his soul, the wellsprings of love and compassion. "The best way to handle scars," Sarah observed, "is to remember things big enough to wipe them out. That's the only way to steer one's course in the world."

Chase wrote *Mary Peters* along with her usual commitments of reading and correcting themes, honoring lecture engagements, attending meetings and answering myriads of phone calls from editors. Her well-worn composition tablet accompanied her on two round trips from coast to coast and on an ocean liner from New York to London and back. It had been opened to receive a few hasty paragraphs in railway depots, lunch rooms and churches, in steamship cabins, and on a snowbound day coach in northern Minnesota. The notebook was retrieved from a mountain stream in New Hampshire and from a wastebasket where a careless maid discarded it. As Chase was penning the last lines of the novel, she was interrupted by a student who wanted to discuss an especially inferior theme. The girl told Chase that her work might have been better if she had a more conducive atmosphere in which to write, a quiet place where she could be inspired. "I'm sure as an author," she said to Chase, "you must know what I mean." "I'm afraid not,"

Chase retorted. "You see, what I consider my best chapter was written in the ladies' room of the Buffalo railroad station at 1 a.m. while a fat cleaning lady slopped the dirty floor with soapsuds and sang lustily, 'Will there be any stars in my crown?'"

Mary Peters had a somewhat checkered history. In November 1933, after completing the first section, Chase wrote Edward Weeks at the *Atlantic Monthly Press*. The magazine sponsored an annual contest for unpublished fiction. Since Chase was one of their favorite contributors, Weeks was eager to read the opening chapters. She informed him that Henry Holt had offered a substantial advance in order to secure the book for themselves. At the same time, Harold Latham, an editor at Macmillan, expressed interest. He proposed a $2,000 advance, sight unseen, and 15 percent royalties, thus outbidding Holt. Chase was in a dilemma; she sought the advice of President Neilson who urged her to go with Macmillan because of their sterling reputation and marketing skills. The firm not only presented a generous contract, but they assured her that they would publish all her works. In late December Chase signed the Macmillan agreement.

Chase implored Weeks to consider her for the prize. However, after perusing the manuscript, he had misgivings about its merits. In an article in the *Atlantic*, he condemned her superficial treatment of the main characters, stating that they were "one-note people": "They can do only one thing—and doing it deprives them both of surprise and sympathy." He also reproached her for not forewarning the reader of unexpected crises.

Other critics praised the book as "magnificent, a social document of lasting value." But it was Weeks' accusation that haunted Chase. She wrote him: "A critic is a critic with the rights of one . . . The whole thesis of my book is against preparation in your sense. I want them to come suddenly, above all else I do not want them to assume undue proportions. You criticize me because I do not arouse 'pity.' But pity is precisely what

I want to avoid. No one of my characters is pitiable. That is just the point. They, the best, are meant to be triumphant . . . Never mind though. Some quiet souls must like *Mary Peters* as I see her on the best seller lists. It's just as well that I didn't [submit her for the prize], for I'd have hated to have her poor head chopped off by your judges."

Mary Peters elicited hundreds of missives from Maine to California. One reader wrote Chase asking for one of her old handkerchiefs as a memento, an Alabaman informed her that pecans were not so "sexually stimulating as roast beef," implying that meat was bad for the creative mind. This correspondent was delighted to supply the pecans, shelled and delivered regularly to Chase's door at four dollars for a five pound bag. The Waterman Fountain Pen Company offered Chase a dozen pens if she would autograph her novel with their product. A gentleman from Texas said it was evident that Chase belonged to no Christian church and that when she met her Maker at the Last Judgment she would have to answer for her pagan comments on life and death. A lady from Oklahoma stated that Shakespeare would "never have been guilty of her repetitious prose," and a Southern school teacher warned her that she could not recommend to her pupils a book which "misuses so many English words." Another woman from Alabama wrote that it was apparent that Chase knew the "love life" and begged to be informed whether she had ever been married, "sacramentally or otherwise." A man from Tanganika Territory informed Chase that he and God were aware that she was living a life of illicit love or else she would have never written the book. This gentleman's statement was justified when the Kennebunk library banned the novel on grounds of indecency. Chase "always had a sneaking desire to live a slightly off-color life, but it seems hard to get the censure without any of the compensations."

Silas Crockett, 1935

With the publication of *Mary Peters*, Chase became recognized as a leading American regional novelist; in England she was in great demand on the social circuit. Her admirers included Doris Leslie, author of the best seller *Full Flavors*, and Charles Morgan, who wrote the popular novel *The Fountainhead*. Although Chase was usually disappointed when she met famous writers, she was charmed by Vera Brittain and Phyllis McGinley. Rose Macauley was "perfectly hair-raising both because she is so clever and so handsome." Chase wished she could flee to some remote island; she was "sick of the nonsense that trails a best seller."

On one of her trips to London, the American Women's Club honored her at an elegant luncheon. At Doris Leslie's cocktail party, fifty authors were present. On another occasion, she autographed 450 copies of *Mary Peters*, had eight photographs taken by various tabloids and dined with editors of the London press. The *Daily News*, Britain's largest newspaper (and in Chase's opinion the most scandalous), chose it for the Book of the Month selection. Chase thought it was strange that her new book, which stressed a quiet life of contemplation, should cause so much excitement.

Burnt Close, her refuge from this commotion, was located in Grantchester, five miles from Cambridge. In January 1935 Chase and Duckett were settled comfortably in their small, staffed cottage. The house, a replica of a sixteenth-century dwelling with tiled roof and beamed black-oak ceilings, had a lovely garden with snowdrops, aconites and irises in bloom. Surrounding the villa were quaint thatched barns, verdant grasslands and smooth, green East Anglian fields. It overlooked the distant towers and spires of Cambridge, those of King's Chapel, the Church of St. Andrew and St. Mary. Over the wall to the south was the spacious expanse of the old Manor Farm; the north afforded a spectacular view of the pinnacles of King's College Chapel.

One of the perquisites of Burnt Close was Mrs. Weightman, a splendid cook and a fastidious housekeeper. Chase's routine suited her perfectly. She arose before seven, prepared breakfast and worked on her new book. It was an ideal situation: she had no domestic responsibilities, no students to teach and long, uninterrupted hours in which to labor. She received more than 150 letters praising *Mary Peters*, and was concerned that she might not have time to answer all of them. She considered hiring a secretary, but feared this would jeopardize her privacy. "It does seem as though one pays dearly for publicity in this world," she wrote her mother. "Aside from the money I hate and despise it all . . . I have offers in every mail for stories and at least a dozen requests for the serial rights of this new book . . . some editors offer between $20,000 and $35,000 . . . I do not want any book published in *Redbook* or *Ladies Home Journal* or any of them, for I think them all second rate, and besides I am making all the money I want or need . . . I want to have my work have a *literary* value, not a mere financial value . . . The minute I get into the popular magazines I shall feel I have taken a step down, and I'm not doing it for mere money."

In February Chase wrote Mable an accurate description of her new novel: "My book has started very well, I think, and I am pleased with it. It is called *Silas Crockett*, and it is the story of Maine seafaring life, also fishing, from 1830 to 1930 . . . It needs a tremendous amount of study and research, and I have been at that all the fall, working over marine reports, shipbuilding, fisheries, etc . . . I try to write 1,000 words a day, sometimes less and sometimes more."

There were many gratifications at Burnt Close: weeding the garden, part ownership of a West Highland terrier named Giles, a library of fine books, and the delightful English countryside in which to roam. On winter days a coal fire blazed in the living room; on cold January nights one could hear the mournful bleating of newborn lambs; and in the spring the cuckoo sang from dawn to dusk. It was in this setting of rich repose that

Chase constructed the powerful Crockett saga, four vividly drawn tableaus of a declining family.

Chase hoped that the book would be valuable as a historical document; as a regionalist, her commitment to the past was inevitable. *Silas Crockett* was her most meticulously documented novel; it highlighted the perplexity of change and the intricacy of inheritance. As the book was nearing completion, Chase wrote an essay explaining that her novel was not a story of consuming plot interest, nor one of elaborate design. In "The Author and His Reader" (*Smith Alumnae Quarterly*, November 1935), Chase noted: "There is description in it of the Maine coast and other lands which . . . contributed to the thoughts and feelings of Maine men and women . . . there are conversations, which . . . are written with a view to the better understanding of my characters . . . The incidents often stand by themselves, are complete in themselves . . . the method of my book has been determined . . . by my very purpose in writing it."

In this compelling story Chase portrayed the maritime life on the coast for one hundred years. She purposely placed more emphasis on setting and character than on plot and incident. There is a direct correlation between the demise of the shipbuilding era and the ultimate downfall of the Crocketts. The saga spans the century from 1830 to 1930, from the time when Silas I, the scion of the legacy, pursued a respectable seafaring profession to the days when his great-grandson, Silas II, was forced to accept a demeaning job in a herring factory. The defeat of the Crocketts is implicit when young Silas visits the old family homestead after it has been sold to a wealthy Philadelphian. It is enclosed within lush, carefully manicured lawns and formal gardens, a golf course has replaced the meadow and the barn had been renovated into a three-car garage. The residence was immaculate, restored and refurbished, but the man who was born and bred there was a stranded outsider.

The novel ends on a note of affirmation as Silas declares that "all the things we've learned can't take away what's rooted in us through generations like these around us and through this coast and sea. Believing in a thing means hanging on to it because you know it's good even though you lose faith in it for a while."

Chase composed the last lines on a sleeping car from Boston to New York in the early hours of September 13, 1935. She always claimed that the best parts of her novels were written in the ladies room on a train; she loved the privacy, light, and convenience of a ten-cent toilet. Although she rarely read her own fiction, the journey gave her ample time to assess the book, and she was gratified with the results. From the Albany terminal she wrote Marion Dodd, manager of the Hampshire Bookshop: "I hope [Silas] is good. I think the last part the best . . . I feel absolutely a different woman since Silas is done, tired as I am."

The reviews surpassed her expectations. The *Boston Transcript* (November 16, 1935) declared that the novel was "an epic of Maine seafaring. It is quite possible that nothing will ever be written which will reveal so clearly the glory and the tragedy which befell the State." John Cheever (*New Republic*, December 11, 1935) observed that "this, to Yankees of the new generation, is a story less for reverence and delicacy, or even melancholy, than for immense indignation and wonder." Lewis Gannett (*New York Herald Tribune*, November 12, 1935) noted that "*Silas Crockett* has the same heart-warming quality [as *Mary Peters*]. It is cut from the same pine log." Robert P.T. Coffin, Maine poet and educator, acclaimed Chase as the most perceptive spokesperson of her state. In a lead article of the November 17, 1935, issue of the *New York Times Book Review*, Stanley Young appraised the chronicle as a "fine page in America's past . . . [Chase] has the gift of understanding disciplined with the gift of selection. With *Silas Crockett* she takes her place among the rarer talents of the present."

Mildred, Mary, Edith, Edward, Jr.—
the first Chase children, c. 1893.

Mary E. Chase, June 1909; graduation
at University of Maine, Orono.

*Edward Everettt Chase and
Newton Kimball Chase, c. 1910*

Mable Lord Chase (Mary's mother)

Mary Ellen Chase, February 14, 1915

Chase residence, Blue Hill, Maine

Blue Hill Bay

ABOVE: *A picnic with friends, c. 1921*

BELOW: *Mary Ellen Chase on horse, c. 1921.*

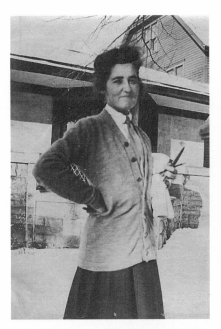

ABOVE LEFT: *Mary Ellen Chase, c. 1926*

ABOVE RIGHT: *Mary Ellen Chase with prize woodchuck, c. 1921*

LEFT: *Mary Ellen Chase and Eleanor Duckett, returning from England aboard the Queen Mary, fall 1961.*
(Smith College Archives, Smith College. George V. Bigelow, Cunard Line, photographer.)

TOP: *Windswept*

CENTER: *Mary Ellen Chase and Dr. Paul Dudley White, c. 1946*

BELOW: *Esther Ziskind Weltman (left) with Mary Ellen Chase, c. 1948*

Mary Ellen Chase, December 1941

CHAPTER ELEVEN

Dawn in Lyonesse
1938

In 1936, when Chase was on sabbatical, she wrote *This England*, a compilation of essays based mainly on ideas and sentiments. This volume represents the peak of her art as an essayist and reveals her profound attachment to England, an allegiance nearly as intense as her love for Maine. She wrote on a variety of topics, mainly on rural life. "An English Sunday" has a trace of irony mingled with praise concerning British manners, the bland food, the traditional Anglican Sunday, and railroad travel. Her style is wholly engaging, mellow, witty and amusing, interspersed with delicate satire. In the southwest corner of the land Chase encountered a friendly, close-knit people living in harmony with their environment. She blends the inhabitants of the region—farmers, fishermen, shepherds—into a landscape that was a decisive force in shaping their lives.

Chase's trips to Cornwall in 1934 and 1936 afforded rich literary material. She went alone with some trepidation, for she did not know if she could weather an entire season by herself. She experienced all the usual anxieties: illness alone, bad news alone, being homesick. But she maintained that "solitary counsels and good tidings are the gifts to self-imposed and self-directed solitude: that confidence in ourselves . . . which can come to us only from our being at times alone."

During the long, relaxing mornings she read on the summit of a cliff above the restless Cornish sea, listening to the rush of the water and the wind whistling through the crevices. On rainy days she sought a haven beneath a jutting rock. When the weather was clear and warm, she took off her shoes and basked in the sun, the breakers below resounding in the still air. She walked through miles of gorse and heather along the ocean paths. She kept daily notes, recording the distinctive qualities of the area, dramatic aspects of the elements, typical Cornish names, local superstitions, indigenous birds and plants. The isolation was so gratifying that she vowed she would not allow a day to pass without spending a portion of it in solitude.

She journeyed to Helford where she was fascinated by the granite sky, misty rain, dark waters, verdant hills, and sloping valleys. It was a rugged stretch of land without hedgerow or meadow, a country of stone, black heather, and stunted brown moorland grass. Long shadows fled across the moors like pointed fingers. The silence on the moors belonged to another age, an era past and vanished as though it had never existed. There were no trees, except one or two that lifted bare branches to the four winds, bent and twisted from centuries of storms. The tors stood out boldly against the hard blue sky, the grass glistened stiff and white, rimed with frost. The only sounds were those of a raven flapping his great black wings. A lone curlew stood pensively by the stream watching his reflection in the water. Then, suddenly, he tucked his legs under him and ascended into the air, streaking for the south.

The windswept coast of Cornwall reminded Chase of the crags, mountains, and sweeping pastures of rural Maine. The landscape presents dramatic contrasts: rock-strewn beaches battered by Atlantic waves; deep, lush coombe where wild flowers bloom all year; high, remote moorland with granite farmhouses; sheltered creeks winding behind wooden banks. Winged furze is everywhere, golden flame-colored blossoms, their brilliance sparkling on the ground. There is the constant motion of gulls, rushing and swooping in the clouds above. The coastline winds for over 150 miles of coves and sandy shores, with clifftops of thrift and thyme. The golden lichen atop the old roofs is an indication of the clean, pure air, and the transparent light is evidence of the variable maritime climate.

At Land's End the contours of the land merge into infinity as Cornwall comes to an abrupt close. Its granite cliffs are carved and buffeted into pointed spires by the full force of the Atlantic; even the sharp, sorrowful cries of the pipit lend a melancholy air to this great expanse. The lost land of Lyonesse, between Land's End and Scillies, was famous in the annals of romance, a realm that disappeared from the map when it was overcome by the ocean. Cornwall provided a vast and somber setting for Chase's novel; it was a land that defied the wants of its denizens and revealed their struggles as inconsequential. In time so long forgotten that memory could not recapture it, lived the lovers Tristram and Iseault.

It was this fascination with the land that prompted Chase to write *Dawn in Lyonesse*. Described by some critics as an "idyll" or "prose poem," the work ranked high in economy of structure and deftness in narrative skill. In the short space of 114 pages, the action taking place within forty-eight hours, the lives of Ellen Pascoe and Susan Pengilly are so well-defined that "their past was clear, their future implicit in the present." For Ellen, days without conscious association are meaningless; she cannot live without her dreams. When she discovers the red book containing the story of Tristram, her life assumes a different perspective; it awakens her mind to the richness of the past and the promise of the future. The legend enhances her drab romance with Derek Tregonny, a sullen lobster trapper whom she plans to marry.

But Ellen's happiness is ephemeral; six weeks before the wedding Derek commits suicide. Following the tragedy, she learns that he was having an affair with her best friend, Susan. Although this discovery threatens to disrupt her life, Ellen, fortified by the Tristram myth, is forgiving. She accepts the death of her lover and her friend's infidelity. Her release into timelessness is now complete. As she views her personal misfortune in the light of the past, she feels pity for Susan rather than hate. Wisdom comes to her "like a dawn that comes on slowly out of an unknown ocean." She is not alone, she is merely enduring the same anguish that man has borne for generations.

Dawn in Lyonesse affirms Chase's belief in the limitless potential of the human soul, that through consciousness of the past, one can experience a spiritual rebirth. The novel's theme is the acquisition of wisdom, the freeing of the mind from the pettiness of the daily round through an awareness of the human lot. The charm and beauty of the book evolves from inner emotions aroused by a contemplation of the past.

Percy Boynton observed that the "characterization is exercised to its highest degree." Perry Westbrook noted that "it is indeed almost a perfect short novel—one that ranks . . . with the very best novelists that American writers have produced—those of James, Melville, and Willa Cather." The *Boston Herald* commented: "It is destined for a permanent place in American literature . . . in rare measures it combines good, honest words for the soul of humanity; it is clean and kind."

Chase wrote Mildred Hillhouse that writing *Dawn in Lyonesse* was "veritable slavery . . . every word counted and there couldn't be one too many without spoiling the thing." All she cared about was that it was fairly well done. The book elicited letters from readers nationwide. A New York podiatrist wrote Chase that if she would send him ten autographed copies he would be honored, as an exchange courtesy, to care for her feet. Another gentleman, apparently of the old school, informed her that as a teacher of the younger generation, she had openly encouraged, aided and abetted immoral living. He said he could hardly bring himself to recognize her writing when her "moral outlook was so faulty."

III.

A Best-Selling Author

CHAPTER TWELVE

Windswept

1940-1941

In January 1940, Chase boarded the North Coast Limited for a midwestern lecture tour. Approaching her fifty-fourth year, she was a handsome woman and an imposing figure. Her somewhat austere features, snow-white hair and expressive light blue eyes, made a striking impression. She wore a stylish gray suit, a magenta blouse with a white ruffled collar, and simple pearl clips adorned her pierced ears. Her lips were tinted ruby red and a trace of humor flickered in her ready smile. Red was her favorite shade, she called it the "color of life." She carried a battered briefcase, bulging with papers, and her affect was that of a competent and self-assured individual, all her energies directed toward clearly defined goals.

After thirty-one years of teaching, half of them at Smith College, Chase was a campus favorite. Students were captivated by her vibrant personality. In the classroom she was a master showman, striding down the aisles, hands on hips, her eyes twinkling, enlivening the worlds of Moll Flanders and Tom Jones. Her voice was deep and resonant, her cultivated British accent, acquired from spending many years in England and living with a Britisher, added a touch of class. Chase, who liked a wide margin in her life, welcomed speaking tours. They released her from the dreary round of academic life and afforded her time to write, to read and to be alone.

Privacy was essential to Chase's well-being. This quest for solitude prompted her to seek a remote, sequestered spot where she could work in peace. In August 1934, on an automobile trip down the rockstrewn coast of Maine, she encountered a region that was startling in its natural beauty. Petit Manan Point, situated between Schoodic and Gouldsboro, was a precipitous headland, cut by the fierce tides, the only sounds those of wind and water. Blueberry fields tumbled down toward the wooded point and the clumps of buffeted spruce trees cast purple shadows in the sunlight. The distant hills of Mount Cadillac sliced through the western sky and the silhouette of Mount Desert was visible even on sunless days. The stark isolation of the terrain and its eerie silence conveyed a sacred quality to the site. Duckett remarked that she detected a bit too much of Wuthering Heights and Egdon Heath in the region, but it suited Chase perfectly. She loved every spike of goldenrod, every red cranberry, every hour of tranquillity. She was convinced that this special place had been designated for her, and in this brief summer visit she was mesmerized by its magic. She could not disengage herself from it, even when absent.

By 1940 the war in Europe restricted Chase's annual trips abroad. At the close of the academic year, she rented the house near Milbridge that she had discovered six years earlier. "Providence has led me here," she noted in her journal, "it is European-Cornwall, Devonshire, the Hebrides, Brittainy, Maine. It has a spell." The gray shingled abode, its tangled grass high with wild strawberries, was surrounded by water. Chase always longed to be near the sea, sounding at night on any wind, dramatic on any tide. The days varied in their still-ness, weeks of clinging fog gave way to brightness when the morning light streamed across the ocean and the plains, turn-ing the color of the sea to a brilliant blue.

The simple country routine was invigorating. Chase arose at dawn to watch the sky transformed to a milky white on cloudy days and a cerulean blue when it was fair. From her vantage point she could distinguish the outlines of several islands, Schoodic Point and majestic Mount Cadillac, clear and lumi-nous even in haze. She spent most of the time alone on the pastures above Bear Cove with Gregory, her frisky West High-land terrier, at her side. As she picked wild berries for breakfast, she felt well and free, detached from the sorrows of the world, desultory in her mind, childlike and young.

Chase named the house "Windswept" because the trees were "bright, windswept, sparse, gaunt from many gales of wind." Her creativity was sparked by the charm of the land. On August 8, while picnicking at Bear Cove, she thought of composing a series of sketches, not for money but to see if she could capture the dis-tinctive qualities of the coast, its European traits and aura of antiquity, its desolation and friendliness. These vignettes formed the core of the novel that she completed the following year.

That summer Chase began work on the book. By August 22 it would not let her rest. At first only the setting was clear, but soon the story began to take shape. Her characters were compos-ites of people she knew, the locale, familiar places she had loved. She wrote steadily in the private wing off her bedroom, spending at least ten hours a day at her desk and often laboring through the night. In January 1941 she wrote her friends, Mathilde and Mike Elliott, that she was so enraptured with her new surround-ings that she had placed her novel there and "lovingly called it Windswept. It is a difficult title to live up to with its Pentecostal connotations—nevertheless, I am writing it with a minor toll of blood, sweat and tears . . . It should be done by June."

The winter of 1941 was darkened by chaos abroad. As the

war escalated, Chase found it hard to concentrate. There were weeks when she wrote nothing at all. Whatever inspiration she had at the outset had vanished from her heart and mind. France had fallen and the British were fighting valiantly to save their country. For the second time in her life, the lights were being extinguished all over Europe. She keenly felt the waste of war, the separation of young men from their families. The world, fragmented as it was, did not seem a fit place to live. The older she grew, the more she felt the need to preserve the positive aspects of the past.

Windswept was her catharsis: total absorption helped her forget the terrifying state of the world. In March she sent the first eighty pages to Harold Latham, her editor at Macmillan. Two weeks later he wrote her a discouraging letter, stating that he was not impressed with what he had read. This was a great disappointment, but Chase was resolute. She revised the first section and on April 27 mailed the revised text to Latham. He sent Chase a $1,000 advance, enclosing a complimentary message. When Chase sent a copy of his letter to her mother, Mable replied: "I just couldn't keep the tears back when I read all those lovely things about the book and to think that I should have a daughter worthy of such praise and able to create characters of such a type as those in the book makes me so proud and happy that I don't know how to express myself to you. A lady said to me that I should be very proud in that you have never lowered your style. Your father would be so proud if he were alive."

By the spring of 1941 the United States was moving inexorably toward war. The news was grim with threats of invasion. Chase wrote Mildred Hillhouse: "After all the tragedy of the familiar is that it is so seldom apprehended and understood, and all the things in my house have become more to me since September 1939." Chase's beloved colleague, the English novelist Helen Simpson, was killed by a bomb in November 1941, and a cherished British acquaintance in the RAF was shot down in October. By 1944 her loved ones were scattered from

Orono to Burma and from Ireland to Italy. Her brother Newton was a second lieutenant stationed in Georgia and her favorite nephew Ted Weren was an ensign in the South Pacific. Two other nephews were in the Air Force and a third in the Coast Artillery. At least a dozen boys from Blue Hill stock and Windswept environs were dead, and to their families, who had never before acknowledged the existence of the South Pacific or Italy, the grief was untold sorrow and bitterness.

Although the consuming gloom of the war dominated Chase's life, she was soothed by the stillness at Windswept. On the afternoon of September 2 she finished the novel. She then drove to a confectionary shop in Milbridge where she sipped two cokes and ate twenty cents worth of chocolate ice cream. That night she went to bed without pencil and paper by her side for the first time in fifteen months.

The following week Latham informed her that he thought the book was "superb." Macmillan increased the first printing to 80,000 and scheduled publication for November 12. "I am sure either the Macmillan Company or the booksellers, or the reading public is quite insane," Chase wrote Mathilde. "The first chapter will tell you whether I've got Petit Manan really or not. Don't read the thing through. It's not worth it." A few days later, Chase escaped to the midwest where book signing parties were held in Chicago and Cleveland. On the train she vowed that she would never write another novel.

Chase was preparing to attend a celebratory luncheon when she stumbled down a flight of steps in the lobby of Chicago's Drake Hotel. Sterling North came to her rescue and drove her to a local hospital. Chase did not know that her arm was broken, and she felt that she could not disappoint Macmillan. The attending physician recommended that she return home immediately, but his dauntless patient continued on to Cleveland with her arm in a sling, making speeches and enjoying gourmet meals. There were Smith girls who, out of love for her, helped her dress, and chambermaids who assisted her for a quarter.

The pain was not acute until she arrived in Northampton with a badly bruised, swollen left hand and arm. Dr. Hayes set the radial fracture and applied a cast for four weeks.

By the end of November sales of the book approached 125,000. One reader wrote Chase that she usually liked her books, but she could not "reconcile their pure tone with the everpresent presence of adultery. Is it wrong of me to presuppose personal experience?" After an initial reading of *Windswept*, Chase noted in her diary: "A book far short of the hopes and dreams of its author." As a perfectionist, she was certain that the novel was flawed, but she loved writing it since it enclosed so much of herself.

Macmillan issued a five page pamphlet praising the novel, stressing the fact that it had been on Chase's mind for years, a novel that "would show the mutual contributions of pioneer and immigrant stock to America and the mutual obligations of these mingled citizens to America and to each other. . . . The result was *Windswept*, the novel now on the lips of everyone who appreciates richness in story, faultless prose, a theme warm with human sympathy, in short, a book one is proud and grateful to have read. . . . The Human Value is the basis of all she writes, and her generous spirit brings cheer and warmth to many hearts."

As Latham travelled from coast to coast promoting the book, he was gratified by its reception. "People all over the country spoke to me about the book," he wrote Chase. "One of the pleasantest experiences of my trip was to be called on the phone or to be buttonholed after a meeting to be told that *Windswept* was the most satisfying book in years." He informed her that even Moe Annenberg, the notorious gambler, requested that a copy be sent to him at the State Penitentiary in Lewisburg.

Claude Feuss, headmaster of Phillips Academy, wrote Chase: "*Windswept* is a truly great book . . . It is quite likely to survive as long as any American novel in the past decade." A poll of critics at *Harper's* placed it first on their list; by January it was still in the lead. The runner-up was A.J. Cronin's *The Keys of the Kingdom*.

Chase received thirty to fifty letters daily extolling her work, but she was still skeptical about its value. She wrote Lewis Gannett: "No one knows so well as I the faults in *Windswept*. All the kind things people say of an author's book cannot erase the sadness of things which one could accomplish, given oneself!" She told Mathilde: "My book drives me crazy. My mail is mountainous and mostly mealy. It doesn't deserve all this nonsense . . . I can't get on a train without seeing the miserable thing or even buy kleenex at Lord & Taylor's without some salesgirl saying did I really write *Windswept*—God knows, I wish I hadn't."

Six weeks after publication the novel was on the top of the best seller lists in the *New York Times* and the *Herald Tribune*. In a lead article in the *New York Times Book Review* (November 16, 1941) Katherine Woods observed: "The essence and reality of life itself is embodied in one of the finest of contemporary novels." For many readers the saga was an escape from the dire war news after the invasion of Pearl Harbor. Many of the letters Chase received were from servicemen on active duty, their families, and hundreds of clergymen.

Windswept made Chase rich and famous; she was able to live quite comfortably on royalties for the rest of her life. By 1952 it was in its fifteenth printing; editions had been published in Britain, in Germany and in Sweden. Aided by the funds from her novel, Chase purchased Windswept, the house and the land. On a snowy, soundless December morning, she wrote a check for $4,500, with "the past on one side and the future on the other." Never had she paid so willingly and with the sense that she was getting "what cannot be bought and sold."

Windswept evolved from Chase's deep feeling for the land. Her characters exhibit a sense of rootedness, a belief that the past is alive as much as the present. She espouses her strong position on the rights of inheritance, the significance of tradition and her faith in man's powers of endurance, his hope and his rationality. She writes of America as a land of promise where the foreigner can fashion a new self-image from the strengths of his legacy. Both the native born and the newcomer need spiritual roots planted firmly in time and place. The settler's most valuable contribution is his awareness of an ongoing culture that he shares with his adopted countrymen.

Although the setting is the Pine Tree State, Chase did not consider *Windswept* one of her Maine novels. The book does not deal primarily with regional issues or with typical Downeasters. The essence of the drama concerns the transplantation of the immigrant to Maine, his adjustment to the land and the beneficial effects resulting from this synthesis. Windswept, a house on the Maine coast, on a high promontory overlooking the sea, is the core of the story. John Marston built it in the early 1880s and made it the cherished center of his families' lives. The book is a chronicle of three generations of Marstons, from 1880 to the eve of World War II.

The novels written after *Mary Peters* and *Silas Crockett* focus on the search for the old virtues that give man some measure of jurisdiction over the turbulence in the world and dignity in the face of the forces he cannot control. *Mary Peters, Silas Crockett,* and *Windswept* are a trilogy in the sense of having a similar theme, that of generational perpetuity. In *Windswept* Chase is more circumspect as she explores the exigencies of life and states her prevailing belief that the only sure foundation for a well-integrated personality is positive childhood memories.

Chase was sanguine about the future of immigrant cultures moving into New York, manning the mills in New England, and occupying many acres of homesteading land. She firmly believed that society thrives only when exposed to variant societies. Sometimes the foreigner's contribution is religious, sometimes a tradition of hard labor and love of the land, but in any case the new country is enriched.

When Philip Marston first saw the rocky headland between Schoodic and Gouldsboro, he knew this site was meant for him. His dream was to build a family manse on a tract of virgin soil for himself and his son John. His partner in this venture is Jan Pisek, a Bohemian whose identity is kept alive by memories of the past. Jan represents the archetypal man, the model of the earth. He is hard-working, reliable, and in harmony with the land: "There was something of the very nature of the land itself in his still figure beneath the whitening sky."

On the day the land deed was signed, Philip was accidentally killed while deer hunting. His last request was that they proceed with the building of the house. Jan assumed the role of surrogate father to John, who inherits the property.

Jan's twin sister, Philomena, served as housekeeper for the Marstons for thirty years. She is the embodiment of Chase's stalwart women who often surpass their male counterparts in strength of character. Philomena belonged "on the earth as a man could never belong, her knees upon it, her bare toes digging into it. . . . " She was the "present, homely and secure, she was the good future, which that past and present made possible."

The novel's main thrust and action revolves around John Marston, an introspective intellectual whose life is shaped by the land. He set his roots deep on lonely, rugged Windswept soil. He believes that "a man's roots matter," that identification with a specific region might serve as "an anchor to windward against the storms of time and chance." Through his work as a translator, he meets his equal in Mother Radegund, an erudite French nun, who agrees that "roots matter terribly in one's life, one's faith, one's country, one's language, one's home." When John visits the Mother Superior at the convent, he meets her niece, Adrienne Chartier. Adrienne dies in childbirth, leaving an infant daughter, Julie, the issue of a French captain she met while serving as an army nurse.

Years later Radegund takes her ten-year-old grandniece to Windswept; she considers it to be the safest place for the child.

She asks John to adopt the girl; she trusts him because he is not complex—"he looks at things as they are and lets them alone." She says he is "like the centurion in the Bible," dependable, loyal, honest.

For Julie it is the land that binds and heals. After Mother Radegund's death, Julie is separated forever from the security and safety of convent life. But, as time progresses, she finds consolation in the healing powers of the land. Her staunchest supporter is Roderick, the Marston's youngest child.

On the last day of August 1939, as Julie, Rod and his sister Ann prepare to celebrate Jan and Philomena's eighty-fourth birthday, the German swastika flutters above the old castle in Prague and the Nazis are sweeping through Europe. But Windswept remains inviolable: "From the headland, as far as [one] could see, the land glowed with patches of scarlet and crimson, rust and gold, above the green and purple sea. The flames of Pentecost, coming with a mighty, rushing wind, still touching men so that they may speak in other tongues than their own, still enabling their sons and daughters to prophesy, their young men to see visions and their old men to dream dreams."

Life's pure flame burns, not only in the hearts of poets, saints and prophets, but in the hearts of men everywhere. The roots grounded in Windswept soil grew into ramifications that gathered diverse societies into the mainstream of a dynamic America. *Windswept* personifies Chase's eternal quest for the meaning of life, the deep secret of the mystery of being: "There are moments in human experience when life seems suddenly to concentrate itself, bringing together in a kind of nucleus . . . all its potentialities and powers, all its gifts and graces, all its knowledge and wisdom. At such moments and hours of inter-mission before the half-apprehended flow of conscious and unconscious experience resumes its baffling course, one is aware of a truce with time, which for the moment has been overtaken and captured, seen, even partially understood."

CHAPTER THIRTEEN

1942-1945

After the completion of *Windswept*, Chase did not have the barren feeling that often accompanies the birth of a book. She was glad that the job was done and that she could pursue other interests. In 1941 she introduced a course which soon became the talk of the campus. "The Bible as Literature," called "Chase's Bible" by her students, was a prerequisite for English majors, for Chase believed that a knowledge of Jewish history was essential to a liberal education. In 1918, during a seminar on the English essay at the University of Minnesota, she was appalled at the lack of biblical knowledge. She never forgot the shocking, albeit amusing, incident that confirmed her opinion. The class was reading "Christ's Hospital," an essay by Charles Lamb. In this article, Lamb referred to a famous Old Testament character, Elisha the Tishbite. Chase asked her pupils if they knew who Elisha was. Suddenly, a glimmer of recognition flashed across the face of a girl in the front row: "Miss Chase, I believe I know. Well, I'm not sure, but wasn't she the heroine in *Uncle Tom's Cabin?*" At Smith Chase discovered the same problem. When she asked the students to complete the line: "I will lift up mine eyes unto the hills," the sole volunteer concluded, "My cup runneth over." Only two out of sixty knew the Second Commandment after Chase had recited the First.

When Chase was young, biblical phrases were household words. They were spoken so often that the Chase children were not aware of their origin. Their rooster was called Abner after the captain of the hosts of King Saul. They had a feisty cow named Jezebel, and when their manners were not acceptable, they were reminded of the forty-two children in the Bible who were devoured by bears when they called the prophet Elisha "Old Bald Head." In Blue Hill the Bible was the source of the rules by which most rural New Englanders lived and a guide as to how they should worship.

Encouraged by the enthusiastic response to her course, Chase was prompted to write *The Bible and the Common Reader* (1944), the first of five provocative studies on the subject. She presented her material primarily as the history of the Hebrews through ages of war and peace, prosperity and decline, until the small country capitulated to the strength of the conquerors.

Chase's proficiency in the field brought her national recognition as a biblical authority. In 1946 Dean Weigle of Yale asked her to assist in the revision of the King James Version. Ten years later she received the Constance Lindsey Skinner Award for recognition of her study in this area as well as noteworthy achievement in the field.

Between 1942 and 1943 Chase composed an occasional chapel talk and sometimes an assignment from the Writer's War Board. Signs of war were all over the campus; Northampton was teeming with uniformed women. With the fall of Singapore and the unending conflict in the Pacific, the future seemed dim. Chase was plagued by physical ailments as well. She had abdominal surgery in April 1943; two weeks later she resumed teaching, but she was too tired to write anything.

She went to Windswept in June for two months. The weather on the Maine coast was dramatic in itself. June was a perpetual cloudburst, and when it was not raining, cold winds and dense fog raced across the blueberry patches like light December snow, restricting warmth and sun. July was ushered in by torrential downpours, but from the fourth to the end of the month the days were clear. Petit Manan was lovely, and the evening star sent paths of light across the sea.

That summer Chase redecorated the house for $2,500. The exterior was painted gray green, the color of the sea on certain southwest winds. In her leisure time she made sixteen pairs of white curtains trimmed with colored embroidery. From the high shore to Bear Cove she could see the white saddle board gleaming in the sun, the spruce trees in perfect alignment. She was very content; she had no other desire except to be granted twenty more years of health and sanity.

In January 1944 when Charles Hill asked Chase to assume the English department chairmanship, she was reluctant to do so. Hill and his colleagues, Newton Arvin and Alfred Fisher, were confident that, under her leadership, there would be less infighting. Chase did not think that a chairman should be chosen on a negative basis, but she weakened under pressure.

She paid a heavy price for her generosity. In the fall of that year, she had some unusual spasms of pain which Dr. Paul White, a prominent Boston cardiologist, confirmed as angina pectoris. He advised her to be cautious for four months. She thought that if illness was unavoidable, a heart ailment was a "good, clean and fairly ethical" disease. She had to curtail all strenuous activity, shovelling snow, laying fires, and splitting wood. This meant that a major part of her life had gone, and she had to find a replacement.

Although she did not want to alarm her family, Chase felt that someone should know about her condition. She wrote her sister Virginia: "I am not overly concerned though somewhat surprised . . . I have had more life in fifty-seven years than most people manage and I have no complaints against Fate, life, or what have you . . . My affairs are in perfect shape and I have no financial worries. Unless the specialist says I can't I shall continue in my usual ways. I hope and pray that I shan't leave this world before Mother does or she would be so upset . . . I have had a swell time in my life and I don't want any heroics over this. If I outlast Mother, that's all I want."

When the seizures showed no signs of abating, Chase contacted White. He said that the most severe attacks were over and assured her that within six months to a year she might be relatively well again. However, he warned her that she must avoid starchy foods, inclement weather, and have only six cigarettes a day instead of her usual twenty.

Chase had boundless energy before her heart attack. A graduate student remarked that she was like Antaeus who gained renewed strength every time he touched the earth. It seemed as though she had hidden reserves of power. She noted in her journal: "I wish that everyone could someday hear what is commonly called 'Bad News' about oneself . . . I do not feel frightened at all—rather quietly surprised and quite calm. I do not feel awfully well, but it doesn't seem to matter . . . I like good clean diseases which can't cause anyone else much trouble at the end—whenever it comes." Although she enjoyed her "slowed-down life," she found it impossible to be "light-hearted . . . I do not know how I have weathered it all, but I have. At least I have managed to keep about and that's all I want."

In April 1945, Chase was strong enough to deliver a series of lectures in the south. Upon her return, she experienced severe pain and weariness. On May 5, in Seelye Hall's ladies room, she was stricken by excruciating chest pains. The realization that she was alone, and apparently leaving this world, was frightening. She gripped the coat hooks until a colleague arrived and called an ambulance. Never had she felt so close to death.

For the first few days nurses sat circumspectly around awaiting the end while their patient read Sir William Rothenstein's *Men and Memories,* longing for Paris more than for the throne of God. During the next six weeks Chase went through a profound personal upheaval, physically and spiritually. She did not have a clear sense of time, but she was aware of a great, engulfing sadness for all mankind, for "all who must miss the shadbush, the sea and never know their meaning." Three weeks later she was transferred to Dickinson Hospital and remained there for a month. The doctor's prognosis was guarded; he predicted that she might live for four years if she was cautious, perhaps more. With vigilant monitoring, proper medication and around-the-clock care, her chances for partial recovery were favorable. This was a shocking pronouncement to Chase, who was not quite sixty and had anticipated many more years of productivity. "Is it worth all the tears and bitterness and prayers and money?" she wrote in her journal. "I doubt it. My mind is sterile, but I memorize a great deal and make myself perfect where imperfect . . . I cry whenever anything happens to please me."

Although anxious about her problematic future, Chase maintained a cheerful demeanor. She wished she could distinguish between illusion and reality. Was she so depressed as she perceived herself to be? Was it faith or hope that was supporting her? If anything comforted her at all, it was hope. She wrote Mathilde: "I can honestly say it's rather fun to live on such close terms with destiny and death, in fact, it's positively exciting . . . I play daily a game of chance and one of skill, and enjoy them both . . . I've had a marvellous sojourn on this planet and I'm devoutly thankful that I've 'burned my candles on both ends.'"

Reading was Chase's chief pleasure, but it was not without its cruel stabs. It seemed that everyone mentioned in papers or magazines was bright-eyed and energetic; the world appeared to be getting younger. Chase could not believe that she was no longer young: "I actually am seventeen in my reactions, suffer much the same agony, like the same sort of persons perhaps with more mature judgment, the same sort of books . . . I am bewildered, because I have never caught up with [time]."

Visions of her summer retreat sustained her. When she awoke each morning at five, the habit of a lifetime, she wished she could be there on that vast stretch of land. It was torture to "long for a place as I long for Windswept. I wonder if many people suffer from it. People I do not long for . . . except for brief intervals of love which rarely lasted." For Chase, Windswept was not only a place, it was her life. Without it she felt like Cathy Earnshaw in *Wuthering Heights,* existing without a soul.

In late June, as Chase began to show signs of improvement, she observed a scene that remained fixed in her mind. Outside her window was a glorious sunset, soft and mellow, with a radiant afterglow. In an adjacent room a family hovered over their dying mother. The patient's teenaged grandson wept silently as he watched the ebbing light of day. The woman's breathing was heavy and labored, her fragile fingers clutched the coverlet, and she was sobbing. Chase was deeply affected, she noted that "the tears of children one bears easily, the tears of the young will be dried in time, but there is no hope for the tears of the old and dying." An hour later Chase heard the hearse approach the hospital and saw the headlights beaming as it carried the deceased woman away. She could not sleep that night, for her thoughts were with the grieving boy. This incident formed the basis for *The Plum Tree*, a book about aging and death. The fact that her mind was not "sterile" lifted her spirits.

By the end of June Chase's sedimentation rate and blood pressure readings were normal, and the EKG results were encouraging. Dr. Hayes insisted that she remain in the hospital another week for rehabilitation, to learn how to climb stairs slowly and sit up for twenty minutes a day. After eight weeks of hospitalization, she was discharged and given permission to go to Windswept. When the doctor told her not to plan any lecture tours or to attend any social gatherings, she accepted the news stoically. "Since I can never again uplift the Hokinson ladies of Kalamazoo and Terre Haute and Lima, Ohio, I'm writing another book by slow stages next winter," she wrote Mathilde. "To be told I can never go to receptions again is Balm and Gilead, 'apples of gold in pictures of silver,' in short, I humbly rate myself as one of the Lord's anointed and I sing Psalms and Te Deums over my lot on this earth. No sinner ever deserved less and got more than I!"

Hayes said that Chase should teach only one class, and she knew that was all she could manage. She was forbidden all the things she loathed: dinner parties, arguments, boring people, cold winds, mince pie, and was allowed to do all the things she loved: spending countless hours alone, puttering about the house, reading for days on end, and seeing only those whom she liked. There was no temptation to split wood, to scrub a floor, or to mow a lawn, all ecstasies forever denied her. She dreaded a world "filled with gloom birds who will either tell me that I burned my candles at both ends, or nag at me when I want to paint a fence."

On June 30 Chase and Duckett went to Windswept, accompanied by their housekeeper, and Anne Martula, an attractive Polish nurse. Upon her arrival she wept, as she knew she would, at the sight of the sea and majestic Mount Cadillac, the cranberry bogs, daisies and buttercups that covered the field. A clinging fog enhanced the serenity of the Point. She spent hours on the edge of Consolation Point, picking blueberries on a pillow and listening to the white throats warbling in the distant woods. The gulls circled the ocean, the tide rolled in, the fog swirled around the summits in wraith-like clouds. She did what is known as "nothing" and found it a mine of riches.

A rare sight on the Point was the appearance of two eagles flying over Bear Cove. Since for some months Chase had been striving to "mount up with wings as eagles" and had merely managed to "walk and not faint," these birds were of great spiritual assistance. The trill of the field sparrows ceased with the rotation of the curlews hovering over the blueberries, the cry of the white throats was plaintive, the hermit thrushes were silent, and the barn swallows circled in the fog and sat by the dozens on the wire fence between the barn and the house. The fireweed was brilliant, vying with the beach pear and early goldenrod, and the heavy seas covered the coast with driftwood. Chase was content, less resentful about her illness, willing to accept her new life.

While she was convalescing, her mother lay grievously ill in Blue Hill. In late July Chase's sister Mildred informed her of Mable's deteriorating condition, suggesting that she come as soon as possible. When Chase arrived at the old manse, she found Mable very fragile, but in "prodigal spirits." She was swept by the cruelty of tarrying death, observing her mother's prolonged suffering was bound to affect the climate of her mind.

The house was clean and lovely and the garden well kept, but she was haunted by the ghosts of the past: "The tears, the sorrows, the thwartings, the bewilderments, the despairs—these with all the amenities, the cares taken, the discipline, the sacrifices." Since there was little Chase could do for her mother, she returned to Windswept. On August 6, the Day of Transfiguration, she wrote in her journal: "Everything is transfigured today by a wonderful, shining light . . . Perfect peace now reigns at Windswept."

August 6 marked the destruction of 60 percent of Hiroshima by the atomic bomb. That night the sky was luminous, black gulls flew high across it, and the sea shimmered with stretches of green, crimson and violet. On August 14 the war was declared officially over. Chase was grateful that she had lived to see the end of the strife. But her happiness was ephemeral. On September 14 Mable slipped away with an unforgettable radiance on her face. Chase wrote Mathilde: "We carried her to the old churchyard by the sea in Blue Hill. . . . The strain and sadness were a bit hard on my old alarm clock inside me; but I am getting rested every hour and shall be all right next week. . . . It is so wonderful to know that she is free and safe that I can only sing a Te Deum and remember how gallant and funny she was up to the very end."

When Chase returned to the Point she wrote the Order of Service for that remarkable woman who baked a cake for her on her birthday no matter where she was and read a chapter a day from one of her books along with a Scripture selection. At the service the choir sang Mable's favorite hymn and Chase read an excerpt from Joshua 1:9.

During the last weeks at Windswept the early September

days were perfection. Every detail was sharpened: the geese flying south, humming birds nesting in the snapdragons, loons calling at dawn. Orion was brilliant at four in the morning when Chase took a glass of port and some crackers to the water's edge to view the slow dawn whitening the late stars. It was the most beneficent of autumns: colorful leaves drifted into the clear sunlight from trees left bare with "all their classical truth and visible rhythm."

Nineteen forty-five was one of the most trying years in Chase's life. She was buffeted by forces that were seemingly impossible to surmount: her near-fatal coronary in May, her mother's death in September, and in October the distressing news that her beloved terrier had an inoperable tumor. But Chase had powers of resiliency that enabled her to rise above adversity. These reversals deepened her character, changed her outlook, and gave her a heightened awareness of man's short span on earth. This tumultuous period marked the onset of a series of physical setbacks, but Chase kept on writing, sometimes to escape the harsh reality of a limited existence.

CHAPTER FOURTEEN

1946-1948

In October 1946, Chase spent a frantic, if amusing, two days with the producer, Thomas Job, who was in the midst of adapting *Dawn in Lyonesse* into a play entitled *Land's End*. Job was a melancholy creature who carried a gold-embossed cane and wore yellow doeskin gloves. These gloves clutched an ample supply of amylnitrate to counteract dizzy spells. Chase attempted to cheer him up with several stiff drinks, but to no avail. Job brought the play with him and, after reading it, Chase recommended that he revise the last scene, which she said made "*Othello* look like *Little Women*." Job told her she knew nothing about the theater, and she admitted that this was true. The critics, who agreed with her appraisal, observed that the finale was disastrous. But Chase sympathized with the pathetic figure who "walks daily with death." He was either protesting that he would perish without the potion, or he was pleading for supplication; the prayers were easy, but she could not understand why he "just can't laugh and gamble on his life."

Land's End opened at the Playhouse in New York on December 11, 1946 and closed after a week. Rosamund Gildes, who reviewed it in *Theatre Arts*, commented that it was overacted and pretentious, with garish costumes and discordant music. Several of Chase's friends who attended the play said that they enjoyed it except for the end. Job informed Chase that he was planning to write another drama for financial reasons, and added that he did not "deserve this at the hands of Fate." She was not overly concerned, for he had made nearly one million dollars on London and New York runs of "Uncle Harry." When Chase was in England in 1947, she noticed Job's obituary in *The Times*. She felt somewhat responsible, for she thought that his distress over the play might have contributed to his death. She discovered later that he had taken his own life.

Chase and Duckett planned to go abroad early in 1947, but the trip was nearly cancelled when Chase contracted the flu, complicated by chest pains and fever. An EKG indicated no further heart damage, but she remained in the infirmary for a month in blissful solitude. To keep her mind occupied, she decided to write a story. She composed *The Plum Tree* in one week, writing quickly with a great flow of words, and was pleased with the results. She submitted the tale to *Good House-keeping*'s college story contest; it won second prize of $3,000. Chase was relieved that it did not merit the highest award, for she would have been "too embarrassed." She shared the proceeds with the infirmary, allocating $1,500 for the purchase of a new EKG machine, the refurbishing of several rooms, and other appurtenances.

Harold Latham urged her to elongate the narrative into book form. The ninety-eight-page novella, published in 1949, did not enhance Chase's reputation. The plot is contrived, the setting is vague, and the drama lacks depth and credibility. The theme is somber, bleak in its outlook; it is the work of an ailing author, obsessed with death. Whereas the short version was effective enough to warrant recognition, the longer account belabors the depressing material. However, the book's popularity astonished everyone, especially the editors at Macmillan.

On February 20 Chase and Duckett embarked on the *Queen Elizabeth*. Their cabins on the "floating Babylonian palace" were spacious with comfortable beds and an elegant bath with fresh tap water. White had told Chase that she must travel first class or stay at home. Since the trip was so expensive, she saved fifteen cents a week by washing her own lingerie, eating beans instead of avocados, and contributing one dollar instead of two to the church offering. She celebrated her sixtieth birthday on board at a lively cocktail party given in her honor.

Five days later they reached the frigid shores of Albion and arrived in Southampton after a prolonged delay due to a dock strike. Having been warned of the inclement weather and shortage of food, they brought a carton of dried fruit, juices, long red flannel underwear, three hot water bags, and innumerable sweaters. Their hired chauffeur was unable to drive them to London since high snowdrifts made the roads impassable. After skidding over icy highways for eight miles on a bus, they arrived at the Grand Hotel in Lyndhurst, where they settled for the night in an unheated chamber with an equally chilly adjoining bathroom.

The Cambridge-bound coach was crowded, the windows rimed with frost, snow squalls swirled outside. As they approached London, the city looked dismal. The few people in the streets were shivering, their faces blue with cold. At the Garden House Hotel they received a warm welcome, with daffodils in their suite, a hot meal, and the sense of being home at last. In the garden blackbirds, thrushes, and robins flitted about, and above the Cam River a flock of starving seagulls searched for a morsel of food. The river was rising and floods threatened to inundate the land.

Despite these hardships, there was never a moment when Chase regretted the trip: "Pound notes fly through the air like apple blossoms in May but with none of this beneficence. I feel like Jezebel every morning and Scheherazade every night." In early March, Edith Chrystal came for tea to schedule Chase's Hebrew lessons. Chrystal, whom Chase had known slightly in the 1930s, was sixtyish, tall and gaunt, distinctly plain, although she had "quality." She looked like Gilbert Stuart's portrait of George Washington. She wore her scanty hair in two odd buns over either temple, which resembled sweetbreads. She was Highland Scotch and said that she would never be able to understand "these English." Chrystal was ecstatic when Chase presented her with a pound of American butter and a pair of nylon hose.

Chase's first lesson was fascinating, but she found the exercises difficult and "wandered through the darkness in search of a Golden Bough." She adored every hour devoted to the labyrinthine tongue of the Children of Israel. As the sessions progressed, they became more complicated; the prenominal suffixes haunted her during sleepless nights. Chrystal, who rarely complimented her students, was amazed at Chase's grasp of the language. Chase's progress was so rapid that in four months she had completed a full year's work. She wrote Mathilde that she was unashamedly proud of herself: "Now I understand the Tower of Babel better than ever before for Hebrew is the most confusing, illogical, irritating and intoxicating of languages and I have loved every hour spent with it. I shall bore my class into speedy death, I am sure, but at least I can teach the Old Testament as I never could before."

That winter, British weather was making headlines across the globe. Palm Sunday was frosty, overcast, and cheerless. There was no sign of spring except for the lovely crocuses struggling to erupt on the college grounds. April brought days of turbulent wind and drenching rain. Stores were forced to close and walking was hazardous. There was nothing to buy and nowhere to buy it. Chase wrote Mathilde: "I can never be sufficiently grateful that we have been here these four months. I am sure there is no soul in starvation, but I am equally sure that there is a peculiar soul in deprivation and discomfort. For when you can't ponder over what you may eat, and when you can't buy anything . . . you find yourself . . . not even thinking about what you might do if you could. And thereupon ensues an odd and quite intoxicating sense of freedom. We really didn't mind the cold of March . . . we went about looking like Lane Bryant 50s and honestly didn't give it a thought. We used to take turns putting our hands under each other's armpits and thrill to the warmth there. All in all, I've had the most wonderful four months of a life filled with wonders."

April 10 marked the first full day of sunshine in over six

weeks. "There are really tears in people's eyes as they greet one another," Chase noted in her journal. "There is more than relief or happiness in their faces—there is a return of Faith. . . . There is a new friendliness abroad on these streets. Reserve is broken down—long queues of people smile and talk. The trees have burst out even in ten hours of sun. The willows are green, the daisies star the grass. The daffodils are bursting out on the banks. Even the dogs leap about rejoicing . . . I never before realized what long, deferred light and warmth can do to the human spirit."

She wrote Daniel Aaron, "This island is, as you say, 'bedevilled.' It doesn't seem possible that Nature could be such a malevolent enemy. When we came, in the worst of it, we were simply beset by thousands of seagulls, flying in from the coast in search of food. They were rapacious beyond words and really terrifying. You felt your liver unsafe whenever you ventured out. They killed thousands of small birds and even hens . . . swooping over them and piercing them in the neck. They stayed throughout the snow and cold and seemed like the Erinyas, Furies—a host of Nemesis—against which it was not possible to contend. The weather was really so monstrous that it was frightening and the winds at night positively terrifying."

By mid-May the gardens were at the height of their splendor. From the late snowdrops to the Canterbury Bells, May and June were ideal: long days, mostly fair, and a whole land in bloom. There was something immeasurably poignant in the flowers blossoming among the tombstones; they enhanced the beauty of the burial grounds where old graves lay near ancient walls. In June Chase and Duckett went to the North Country; the region brought promises of cool winds, Doric simplicities, and Roman ruins. In the moorlands was the setting of *Wuthering Heights* in great, rolling reaches of land. They stopped at Haworth, a gray and somber village where the Brontë sisters and their brother Bramwell lived and worked. Emily and Charlotte, with all the other Brontës except Anne, were buried at Scarborough under the stones of the bare church. The graves were so close together that grass could barely grow between them.

At the beginning of August Chase had her final Hebrew lesson. The language still thrilled her. "I have done nothing that I should have done for four months," she wrote Mathilde. "I have neither written letters nor read noble books nor repented of my sins, nor been solicitous of my fellow men, nor mended my tattered garments, nor developed my aging character, nor given up smoking or ceased to drink very bad and very scarce cocktails. But I have been so serene and tranquil in my mind that mere happiness has faded out of sight. I have met West African princes, who believe in polygamy quite sensibly, have lain in cowslips (not with the polygamous princes!), and listened to the cuckoo, studied the habits of snails and mallard ducks and on wet days read the Milton manuscripts in the Trinity Library, dined quietly and scantily with a few very nice people, talked with farmers battling the floods in the fens, smelled the lime trees now in blossom, sat under cold walls in the blessed sun of April after six weeks of cold and rain and snow, and every minute has been mine in a way it has never been before—except at Windswept."

August 5 concluded their stay in Cambridge, a very sad occasion with a farewell cup of tea, the last pound notes left in the dining room. Their empty suitcases were filled with newspapers since they had donated their clothes to the flood-stricken Britishers: "St. Martin of Tours should be my buddy in the next world . . . I have presented my one evening dress to the Mistress of Jesus, Newnham dons sleep in our pajamas, we cut up all our slips to make undervests for various learned and naked females, and we have but two pair of pants each."

When they left Southampton they were teary-eyed. The light was soft and mellow and as they followed the south coast they glimpsed yellow harvest fields. Every day on board Chase transcribed Hebrew; its spell still held her. When they arrived in New York on August 15, they replenished their depleted wardrobe. It was the hottest day on record in forty years. The stifling heat was alleviated only by thoughts of their impending visit to Windswept.

While she was at her summer retreat Chase and Duckett received notification from Natalie Starr informing them that, to honor their many years of service at Smith, a $10,000 scholarship had been established in their names. The Chase-Duckett Scholarship was initiated by Starr, Florence Snow, Florence Adams, class of 1905, and her daughter Jane Adams, class of 1935. The women were thrilled by this sudden immortality accorded them. The unrestricted endowment increased to approximately $70,000 over a period of thirty-five years.

¶

When Chase returned to Smith in the fall she was ready to start the Jonathan Fisher biography. She wrote Mildred: "I shall live chastely yet passionately with him this autumn and he could be resurrected by . . . Christmas. . . . I am very well indeed, and, although I consider mere happiness a rather superficial and over-estimated state, I am vastly content and as serene as one can be."

The Christmas season was marked by a crippling Northeast blizzard. Christmas Day was picturesque with deep snow and cold dry air, and at night shadows from the moon crossed the dark ravine. Her little terrier, Greggy, was very excited over what Chase feared would be his last holiday on this earth. He was "deafer than Beethoven, blinder than Homer, but more faithful than Argus." She gave him a ball, a squeaky toy, and a red bow to adorn his collar. That day, Natalie Starr announced her engagement to Raymond Putman, Smith's professor of music, a forty-nine "hitherto settled bachelor and a most temperamental, though entirely lovely, musician."

Nineteen forty-eight was ushered in on a joyous note with Natalie's marriage on January 7th. Chase and the bride had been intimate friends since 1933. For two days prior to the wedding, she baked nut bread and cookies, arranged sweetheart roses in Natalie's room, and placed white roses on the church altar. On the eve of the ceremony the radiant couple dined with Chase and Duckett. Chase prepared a delectable meal of cold chicken, tossed salad, ice cream, cookies and white Bordeaux wine. The table was lovely with white candles and with a yellow ribbon tied around the wine bottle. At midnight Chase and Natalie savored a last cigarette alone in Chase's room where they had smoked so many in the past.

After the festivities, Chase worked on the Fisher book. Between January 9 and the 19 she wrote 50,000 words. "I really prayed in the early morning to finish this book," she noted in her diary. "My faith, always feeble, was, I cannot say, made stronger by these orisons, but they were both direct and sincere. I cannot bear not to complete this job which, I think, fairly good."

From September 1947 to the end of the year, Chase made no diary entries and wrote few letters. Jonathan Fisher was the reason for her silence. Although Fisher died twenty years before Chase's birth, his influence in Blue Hill was everlasting. He set the pace for its spiritual, moral, political, and social existence. His life and his work hold places of honor in the annals of Maine lore. Despite the fact that the Calvinist authority has ceased, his name still evokes curiosity and wonder.

Jonathan Fisher: Maine Parson 1768-1847 is based on Fisher's "Common Journals," which he kept for forty-five years, and on his countless letters and sermons. Chase's study of this controversial minister is one of her major regional works. In the *San Francisco Chronicle* (November 15, 1948), J.H. Jackson noted that "Chase has rescued from oblivion a human being worth knowing and has done it gracefully and with a full measure of charm. The book commemorates an honest and daring man whose perception of life redeemed his day and generation. It is a credible re-creation of an era in American history."

Although Chase found little levity in the parson, she loved

the story that one morning in 1796, shortly before his marriage to Dolly Battle, Fisher was standing on the roof of his new parsonage, hammer in hand, when a passerby asked him how he was. Raising himself as high as possible on his precarious perch and brandishing his hammer aloft, he answered, "I am preparing for Battle."

Chase wrote Mathilde: "The accounts of the moral life in the early Blue Hill annals make *Forever Amber* look like *Little Women* or the New England Primer! Jonathan told all in the *Church Records* and, believe me, fornication has reached a high artistic standard. I am having some trouble, with Boston near at hand with discreet phraseology! One young man in good standing in the House of God, Joshua Wood by name, is excommunicated in 1806 for his habit of 'pulling up female garments while still on!' The arts of fornication practiced by one Molly Clay . . . would have made Hollywood look like a Baptist prayer meeting—and one Mr. Savage, a deacon of the church . . . was caught in adultery with an Indian Squaw! Not a dull moment with this book." Fornication was so extensive that Fisher composed a form letter listing the cases of excommunication for that transgression.

Fisher voiced his Calvinist warnings to the "erring minds and sinsick souls" of his congregation, but he was aware of human frailty in other areas. He was concerned with the plight of the American Indian as well as the injustice of slavery. He was an ardent spokesman for the American Society for the Colonization of Liberia, an opponent of the War of 1812, and a staunch supporter of the temperance movement, which resulted in the formation of the Blue Hill Temperance Society in 1829.

The parson's missionary journeys continued throughout his life. In 1801 he walked more than three hundred miles across the Maine countryside. He was later employed by the Maine Missionary Society of Sedgwick and Brooksville and went there several times a year, always on foot.

In 1836, toward the end of his forty-three year pastorate in

Blue Hill, the reverend wrote his children: "My attachment to the world has been, and still is, too strong. God's purpose may be to attenuate the ties that hold me to it." The afterworld was Fisher's guide and he was only marking time until he was called to the "real life beyond the grave."

Twenty-year-old Eliza Wescott sang in the choir at Fisher's funeral. She never forgot that day, nor did she ever cease to tell her granddaughter Mary about it. The church was overflowing with people from all over the countryside, from adjacent towns and the outer islands. They stood on the steps and in the fields, listening through the open windows of the church: "Boats filled the harbor; horses and wagons lined the long hill on either side; and yokes of oxen were freed from their carts to crop the roadside grass. And after it was over, all formed in a long procession to follow on foot the parson to his grave."

To immortalize Fisher's love for the ancient sages, the townspeople placed a monument on his grave as a token of respect. On the tall granite shaft, which bears an open book, is Socrates' dictum: "Know thyself." The parson is interred in Blue Hill's Old Burying Ground, where young Mary Chase often went with her friends to gather strawberries. But they did not dare disturb the fruit surrounding the sacred plot.

CHAPTER FIFTEEN

The Rockefeller Friendship
1949-1950

At a special faculty meeting on March 15, 1949, Benjamin Fletcher Wright was named president of Smith College, succeeding Herbert L. Davis, who resigned to pursue scholarly endeavors. The following October, Wright presented Chase with her fifth honorary degree. She was honored along with twelve other distinguished women, including Eleanor Roosevelt, Queen Wilhelmina of the Netherlands, Senator Margaret Chase Smith of Maine, and Sarah Gibson Blanding, Vassar's first female president. Chase wrote Florence Snow: "It is a bit absurd to consider me a 'distinguished literary figure,' as I am anything but that. Being merely a very human creature, however, and very deeply touched, my inadequately expressed thanks to all who have so graciously mistaken my value."

Nineteen forty-nine was rewarding in terms of friendship; Chase renewed her acquaintance with Dorothy Blair, who had been a student in Bozeman in 1916. Her recollection of Blair as a little girl in a red coat amidst the snows of Montana was "one of those radiant, visual memories which stabilize and enliven life, one of those odd, real moments." During that period Chase established an unusual alliance with the Rockefeller family, which resulted in her congenial biography of Abby Aldrich Rockefeller.

On February 7 Chase received a letter from John D. Rockefeller, Jr., inviting her for dinner in New York. He wanted to discuss a proposed biography of his wife, who died the previous spring. Chase was recommended for the assignment by Elizabeth Cutter Morrow and Mackenzie King, Canada's former

Prime Minister. Other candidates under consideration were Anne Morrow Lindbergh, Catherine Drinker Bowen, and Dorothy Canfield Fisher. But Chase was the family favorite since Abby had loved *Windswept*.

Chase never forgot that chilly evening at 740 Park Avenue when her host tenderly draped her shoulders with an eiderdown comforter as an icy wind blew through the bedroom window. He showed her several photos of his late wife and told her of his "dear lady's beauty, her ethical standards, and her consummate charm." He said that everyone who knew her was captivated by her "sweet, genuine friendliness" and her concern for mankind.

Chase spent a disquieting day pondering over the book and thinking of the man who intrigued her. She had many reservations, but was drawn to it mostly because JDR was so appealing. She decided to do it since Blair had consented to be her research assistant, and because she thought it was "in her stars." She was pleasantly surprised when her Smith colleagues endorsed the project.

On April 12 Chase wrote in her journal: "A great happiness is constantly with me. All has worked out for the Rockefeller book. . . . What have I done to deserve such blessings?" She admitted the real reason for accepting the offer in a letter to JDR: "That reason was curiosity—a curiosity in part dictated by my own opinions and principles. At that time you meant nothing to me except the richest man in the world who had used his wealth for the betterment of the human family. I had some misgivings about wealth such as yours, regardless of its use in and for the world. . . . I came to New York to see what you were like. I found you the most simple, sincere, genuine and 'liberal' of men. I liked and admired you so much that fateful evening that I could not possibly refuse your request. Whatever I had thought of great wealth, the owner of it and its steward was the most complete democrat in outlook that I knew, and a man for whom I could have nothing but admiration and trust."

Chase wrote Mathilde that JDR was the most "incredible man I have ever known, so sincere on the one hand, that you can't believe it and so devastatingly keen and witty on the other, that the combination is overpowering. . . . 'Maecenas,' as I call him, is really a charming, sincere, intelligent, and shy creature, whom I vastly like and who fills my irritated hours with merriment heretofore unknown in my rather rich existence."

The remuneration for the book was clear from the start. Chase would receive an aggregate payment of $15,000; this sum included a $5,000 advance and all expenses incurred during the writing of the book. The serialization in *Good Housekeeping*, scheduled for June and July 1950, would realize an additional $10,000. The condensation was expected to attract two or three million readers.

Chase wrote Mildred Hillhouse, explaining that the book was not funded by the Rockefellers: "I tell you this because I know that people will think this is a subsidized book . . . Nothing could be farther from the truth. Mr. Rockefeller has paid me for my time only, generously but not excessively . . . I have not written the book for money, and I have an almost pathetic desire for my best friends to understand that . . . I do not believe in private and uncontrolled holdings of great fortunes; and I could not honestly write a book of this sort, were I being paid a large sum . . . I tell you these things . . . for I want you to know about them, not only for my sake, but for his . . . It is my own, and I alone am responsible for it."

At first Chase's feelings for JDR were purely platonic, but by the summer she had become emotionally involved with him. In July he invited her for a weekend at his eighty-one room "humble cottage," The Eyrie in Seal Harbor. A motor accident en route, caused by a drunken driver who forced Chase's car into a ditch, resulted in a broken rib. Chase spent several days recuperating at The Eyrie. She wrote Mathilde: "A broken rib and JDR, Jr., is a combination which few women have weathered

. . . it was all so incredible and amusing that I quite forgot about the severed rib."

On January 29, 1950, the scion's seventy-fifth birthday, Blair and Chase were invited to dinner at the Park Avenue penthouse, along with twelve family members. The modest menu consisted of pea soup, roast beef, Waldorf salad, chocolate ice cream, and cookies. The host delivered a long and rather touching grace, praying for his wife's soul, asking his guests not to forget those in need, pleading for world peace. After the meal they discussed the book, notably the method of serialization. The family agreed that Chase should have the final decision on editing. They deliberated on the binding; most preferred red for the jacket. The boys opted for Abby's wedding picture; this suggestion was tacitly opposed by Chase. At 9:30 JDR told the clan to leave, since he and his guests were going to Williamsburg the next morning.

On the ride to Williamsburg, Chase drove with Arthur, the family's black chauffeur, whom she found very appealing in his devotion to Abby, especially on behalf of her work for his people. Bassett Hall, where Chase and Blair stayed, was a charming white house, surrounded by ailanthus and elm trees. The daffodils were in bloom and behind the house were carefully trimmed lawns and gardens, bordered by mulberry and holly bushes.

The following day they visited the Ludwell-Paradise House. Chase was amused when the affluent scion, who had already spent fifty million dollars for restoration, bought three tickets at three dollars apiece and had them validated at every landmark. In a letter to Chase after the tour, JDR wrote: "Your manners are not only charming but perfect. Nothing you may say can alter the conviction, long since established on that score by what you do. . . . The informal association between you and Miss Blair made closer the bonds between us all. May the unseen powers that have been helping and guiding you during these past months continue to give you inspiration which has resulted thus far in such an exquisite word picture of the dear lady, my adoration of whom throughout life you can better understand and are even sharing to a degree."

¶

JDR was persistent in his demands for precision and his "feeling or lack of it, for words and their ways in English speech." He told Chase that he was "consumed, even devoured" by her "incredibly beautiful chapters," but requested a conference over words he did not fully understand. Yet, he added, "the book is so perfect as it is and is so more than satisfying, that the question of the addition of even a word to it is relatively unimportant."

Chase was furious when JDR interfered in the serialization. She felt that he was underhanded in his dealings with Macmillan and the *Good Housekeeping* editors, but he protested that this was not true. However, he did attempt to contact Edith Haggard of Curtis Brown, who was indisposed, and was directed to Alan Collins, the firm's president. Collins consulted with the magazine's head, Herbert Mayes, who stated that any cuts would be deletions, rather than changes. Subsequently, JDR phoned Harold Latham to determine whether Chase's contract stipulated condensation in less than three installments. The irate Macmillan editor told him that he was not concerned with the number of installments, but with the amount of deletions. This would enable Latham to stress the fact that, when he published his volume on September 19, 1950, it alone contained the unabridged text.

When Chase received a ten-page advisory letter from JDR regarding these conversations, she was so upset that she went to bed for the rest of the day. She warned him that he was not managing *Good Housekeeping,* Macmillan, or herself. JDR apologized profusely for his innocent intervention: "The book is your book; that gives it its great value. It would have less weight if you had not always had . . . the final decision and the final responsibility in all questions pertaining to it. . . . If these talks with your publishers have given any of these gentlemen to feel that your manuscript was not wholly and solely yours and what was done with it your responsibility, I am most regretful."

The long-awaited publication of *Good Housekeeping*'s June issue was greeted by a receptive audience. Mayes presented the story eloquently, in a manner that commanded the reader's full attention. When the second installment appeared, JDR paid Chase the highest compliment: "With you, as with Mrs. Rockefeller, it is that beautiful quality which makes everyone love you. I wish you could know how much your coming into the lives of the Rockefeller family has meant to us all this past year and how greatly you have enriched our lives."

These heartfelt sentiments moved Chase profoundly and she told him he was a loyal friend. She said that whenever she was discouraged, she thought of him. He replied that she set before him a standard that was difficult to live up to: "Never did I dream that I personally was a factor in your decision to write the story . . . While you, yourself, are the chief reason we have gotten on so well together, perhaps the next most important reason is that you have so many of Mrs. Rockefeller's lovely and winsome qualities."

After Chase explored the relevant facts of Abby's life, the actual writing went quickly. She taught as usual but her mind was always on the Rockefeller book. She was sure that some mysterious force spurred her on. Begun at midnight on July 1, 1949, at the Bellevue Hotel, through weeks of heat and high wind at Petit Manan Point and endless busy days, the last chapter was written in less than three hours at the Chatham Hotel on February 12, 1950.

Abington was Chase's refuge during this whirlwind of activity. Blair's charming clapboard house, built in 1830, had broad floor boards, small mantles, old fireplaces, and antique furniture. It was situated in an isolated Connecticut valley, surrounded by stone walls. The solitude was necessary, invaluable, and lovely. Chase worked all morning, first at the kitchen table, drinking countless cups of coffee. Then she moved to the dining room where a blazing fire warmed her. In the afternoon, after napping for two hours, she strolled along the rustic roads, returning in time for cocktails and supper. Her sense of contentment was surprisingly not at variance with the terrible pressure of words: discovered, selected, set down. She experienced hours of complete exhaustion alternating with periods of exuberance, words tumbling into her head and out. As she reconstructed Abby's life, she realized that she was "a marvellous creature and one of the most attractive women of all time."

During their collaboration on the book, Chase and Blair became lovers; Blair was forty-five, Chase sixty-three. Duckett's research in the Cambridge library during the winter of 1949 afforded sufficient time to intensify their relationship. They planned to meet in April 1950, a rendezvous which filled Duckett with envy. Chase had no guilt feelings; as she grew older, she was attracted to younger women. Chase was captivated by Blair's astute mind and sunny disposition. But she would never leave Duckett for another woman.

Chase met Blair in Southampton on April 20. They spent seven glorious weeks together, a period Chase referred to as the "New Experiment." In her journal she noted: "It is already rewarding to me. This, for her, is what I have wanted and even prayed for . . . All the shadows of yesterday have flown away."

They travelled to Bodmin Moor, Devon and Tintagel, through the Cornish countryside. After eight days of dismal weather in Edinburgh, they boarded the train for Cambridge. They bolted the door of their private compartment because they were terrified of being discovered. From Cambridge, they continued on to London, basked in the sun at Trafalgar Square, observed the spraying fountains and the flock of pigeons flying around the Nelson monument in dark rhythms, cutting the air into curves against the light.

On June 8 Blair returned to the States; Chase remained in

Cambridge. "Neither of us will ever forget [the seven weeks]," Chase wrote in her diary. "[They] will always be borne within us. They have meant everything to me and I know they have meant the same to her." In early July Chase and Duckett embarked on the *Mauretania,* three weeks earlier than scheduled. They arrived in Northampton on July 12; six days later Chase had hemorrhoidal surgery. The physician administered a spinal anesthetic, the safest measure considering her heart condition.

In her journal, Chase noted that the post-operative discomfort was inconsequential compared to the "invasion of places that belong to oneself, the really awful intrusions, even the putting out of one's spirit, reducing it to a pile of gray ashes which can't be fanned alive to glow again . . . no amount of time can ever dim the degradation, humiliation, ignominy of this most loathsome of human experiences." Not even JDR's exquisite bouquet of flowers, visits from concerned friends and the kindness of the staff, could lift the dark curtain from her soul.

During the ensuing weeks Chase had excruciating headaches that showed no signs of abating. She had two frightening incidents: she fell on the kitchen floor in front of the oven, on another occasion she was hurled from her chair and landed four feet away. Chase spent the afternoon of November 10 with a staff of specialists, trying to ascertain the reason for these spells. The doctors advised her to contact Paul White at Massachusetts General Hospital as soon as possible. White concluded that the blackouts indicated arterial blockage; the headaches were an aftereffect of the anesthetic. This was the first major physical setback since her coronary in 1945, and Chase seriously considered retiring earlier than planned.

Chase met JDR once more before they terminated their relationship. In July 1951 a chauffeured Cadillac took her to The Eyrie for the weekend. She would return in her own Dodge Wayfarer. Chase advised her driver, a Smith senior, not to fill the tank, but to leave it discreetly half empty. She knew that it would be replenished with Standard Oil's best gas, washed, polished and lubricated. Chase relaxed in her elegant quarters, a snifter of brandy at her side. She was fascinated by the array of bells next to her bed and longed to press them all.

This visit, which she had anticipated eagerly, ended in bitter disappointment. Although JDR's letters to her were sometimes authoritative, at other times paternal, they conveyed a subtle hint of romance. Her fantasy was that he would propose to her and that she would, of course, politely refuse.

That day Chase observed that her host was unusually quiet and preoccupied. When he took her for a ride through the countryside, he spoke confidentially of his new love. Like a "distressed Samson," he told her "all his heart." He had decided to marry Mrs. Arthur Allen, the widow of his college classmate. When Chase discovered that he had investigated the twenty-four hour marriage license law in Rhode Island, and that he had seen Martha repeatedly in intense meetings, she told him that if he was serious about marriage, he should do it soon.

John and Martha were wed in early September. The following week Chase met the bride with "critical faculties well sharpened." She found Martha to be "completely charming, unassuming, quiet, kind, courteous, easy. She has large and beautiful gray eyes and is lovely to look at. They are very happy and I rejoice." JDR seemed to be flourishing. "I can see no signs in him of Time's inroads," she wrote Mathilde, "[the only difference is that] he does part his hair now on the left side instead of on the right."

IV.

The Nineteen Fifties

CHAPTER SIXTEEN

1952-1954

Chase began her second Bible study, *Readings from the Bible*, in July 1951 and completed it the following January. Windswept was an ideal writer's haven. She usually wrote in her bedroom study and labored most of the day. She loved the early morning; she arose at five to see the last star fade in a brilliant eastern sky. She donned her rubbers, regardless of the weather, strolled about the house, tested the wind, observed the progress of the flowers in the window boxes. Then she went inside, lit the stove and prepared breakfast. The nights were soft and still, the evening star luminous, and the reflection of the full moon on the water transformed Bear Cove into a lake of gold.

The 1950s were fruitful in terms of literary output and national acclaim. At the beginning of the decade, Chase had to her credit the Rockefeller biography, two Bible studies and many eye-catching essays. During this time she was the recipient of several honors: the Sarah Josepha Hale Award, Constance Lindsey Skinner Award, Women's National Book Association Award, Independent Schools Award, Secondary

Education School Board Award for *The Edge of Darkness,* and the Woman of Achievement Award from the University of Minnesota. She could not attend the ceremony for the latter, since she had the flu and the doctor forbade travel. Chase did not think she merited distinction of any kind; she wrote President Morrill expressing her thanks, but suggested he find a more worthy recipient. She admitted that she preferred sitting alone in her quiet house watching the rain falling on the daffodils than being acclaimed as a celebrity. "What would I do with the medal," she wrote Mathilde Elliott, "unless I used it for a hot dish?" The period was also one of transition: in 1954 Chase boldly left Macmillan for a smaller firm, W.W. Norton.

The older she grew, the more she turned to immutable things: the snow lining the dark trees behind her house, the close silver sky, the curves above the black brook. She discovered that the greatest tragedy in life was not in disaster or death or disappointment, but in the "awful revelation that people in whom you have staked much fail you, not in what they say or do to you, but in what you see they do not live by." She wrote Dan Aaron that it was "much easier for older people to be honest than younger," since one "wants, almost desperately at times, to live one's last years in a kind of order and decency and courage. In order partially to do that, one has to be honest, first of all. I know I feel that way about my own, though I'm not doing the job with them that I wish I were." Chase agreed with Job, that the mystery of life enhanced its value, but she was equally sure that there was nothing so heartbreaking as "the pretense and the pride which we have to summon up in order to live through the last days of it."

In February 1952 President Wright asked her to agree on an indefinite leave of absence instead of retiring. This request caught her off guard, for she thought the matter had been resolved. Chase deferred to the president's wishes and proposed an extended vacation for most of 1953. She planned a three-month Mediterranean trip to commence the following January.

Nineteen fifty-two was costly in terms of personal sorrow. In January Chase's brother John had a serious coronary attack; meanwhile, her sister Olive was slowly recuperating from a third cancer operation. At the end of the academic year, Chase went to Windswept to be near Olive. On May 18 Edward informed her that Olive was failing rapidly. On May 24 Olive died, the first of Chase's siblings to go. Chase was not well enough to attend the funeral; she wrote Mathilde that she was "getting used to these bonds, like St. Paul."

Five days later Chase and Duckett sailed for England to attend Duckett's delayed degree ceremony. This award, scheduled for 1951, was postponed due to a technicality. They arrived in London on June 6, a misty day with all the familiar sights: dog roses, golden chains in full bloom, poppies in the wheat, hedge rows, country church towers. When they reached the Garden House Hotel a week later, Cambridge was at the height of its splendor. The island was brimming with roses and the weather was ideal.

June 18, Duckett's great day, dawned in drizzle but cleared by noon. At precisely 2 P.M., she was escorted to her chair by the proctors, looking very distinguished in her black gown. The trembling honoree walked towards Bruce Dickens, an imposing figure in his scarlet cape and fur collar. In sonorous and slightly halting Latin, he directed her to the Vice Chancellor's seat where she knelt, her hands entwined in his. She performed admirably, with grace and shyness mingling. Then she left briefly to don a scarlet robe and returned to the Doctor's bench amidst thundering applause.

Chase described the ceremony in a letter to Dan Aaron: "It was all very medieval and impressive with Latin rolling about the old Senate House and the candidate much excited and very handsome as she knelt and bowed. As for me, I wept quite obviously, I fear, from my high seat above the Vice Chancellor's dais. For I know better than anyone else what meaning it held for her and what a lifetime of study it rewarded. She is a wonderful person, as I have known for twenty-three years, and the world she lives in is just the right one for her though it could never do for me. She is truly without envy, or guile, or suspicion, and she was like an astonished and rapturous child over that degree and over the kindness and admiration of her Cambridge friends."

Chase left Cambridge in late June; Duckett remained in England to continue her research. Shortly thereafter, Chase and Blair went to Windswept. When Blair left on August 1st, Chase was alone during the day, but spent the nights with her neighbors, Father Andrew Mayer and his wife Isabel. Mayer, a Philadelphian, was imported to Pigeon Hill on Chase's suggestion because "his ways with the Almighty" thrilled her. The attractive young pastor was "one of the rarely lovely souls on this planet—so simple and kind that he seemed untouched by the mark and dust which most of us inherit from the start." Long before he approached the altar, he had every man, woman and child adoring him, and the chapel was overflowing with admiring villagers. Chase believed that he was "St. Francis reincarnated"; she had never heard "such simplicity and goodness uttered, and I felt tears spring to my eyes every time I heard him."

❧

Due to a crippling sciatic nerve in her left side and arm, Chase made few journal entries in 1953. Her letters to friends were disclosive, but barely legible. Dr. White told her there was little she could do to ease the pain aside from heating pads and ultra-violet rays. He said that the condition could persist for months and urged her to avoid the harsh New England winter. He recommended a trip to Southern France, Spain, and Italy. His reasons were both therapeutic and self-serving: if she went to Cannes she could meet the Aga Khan, a former patient of his, and, at the same time, do a bit of medical sleuthing. In 1950 White had consulted with the Aga's physicians in India concerning his heart ailment, and while there he had spent several delightful hours with the monarch.

On November 17 Chase and Blair embarked on the S.S. *Constitution*. They spent two months touring the French countryside, and on February 2, slightly jittery and dressed in their "poor best," they drove to the Villa Yabymour. The Aga's palatial residence, situated in the Maritime Alps 2,000 feet above sea level, was a long, flat structure of white stucco. Three French servants unlatched the tall iron gates which opened into a circular path bordered by cypress trees and blossoming azaleas. An elderly maid escorted them into a long, wide hall to an even longer living room, with large windows overlooking the coastline from the Estoril Rock to Cap d'Antibes and the distant Mediterranean horizon. The sun was bright, but low, affording a spectacular view of the Riviera. It was the most exotic place Chase had ever seen.

The visitors found their eminent host reclining in an oversized, plush leather chair. He rose to greet them and spoke fluent English. He was quite old, gentle, not really obese though round and flaccid, with a mane of white hair brushed straight back, brown eyes with slightly askew horn-rimmed spectacles, a full mouth revealing crooked teeth, and a Western rather than an Oriental complexion. He was dressed in a rumpled gray flannel suit, a white shirt, navy tie, and black felt slippers. When Chase asked him the source of his perfect English, he attributed it to the Jesuits in Bombay where he had been educated. He was congenial, but unsophisticated in his knowledge of the United States. He had visited the country only once, in 1906, when he was "shaken to bits" during the San Francisco earthquake. Chase was certain that he had never heard of Smith College, although he asked her what courses she taught and whether the Koran was included.

The Aga's fifth wife, the Begum, joined them. Chase was impressed with her: she was about forty-five, tall and stately, with dark eyes, perfectly coiffed black hair, and light, creamy skin, and she spoke perfect English. She wore a simple, stylish gray wool frock with no jewelry except small diamond earrings that reminded Chase of a pair of clips she had bought at Woolworth's for a dollar. Chase, who was always grading people in and out of class, accorded the Begum an A+, the Aga an A−.

After the Aga expressed his high regard for Dr. White, he engaged in three topics of conversation: his hatred of imperialism in any form (including some comments on Egyptian politics with indiscreet references to King Farouk), his interest in linguistics, and his zealous preoccupation with religion. He offered a protracted explanation of the Moslem idea of God as compared with the Hebrew and Christian concepts, recited some chapters from the Koran, and delved deeply into the Moslem interpretation of time and the creation.

Chase hoped to hear more gossip about King Farouk, but their talk was interrupted by the sudden appearance of the Iranian ambassador to the United States. This somewhat drab individual, who spoke not a word of English, introduced one significant detail: upon his entrance he placed his hands within the Aga's and lowered his head, murmuring something in Arabic that appeared to have a religious connotation. Aside from that, he was an annoying intruder who discouraged the royal couple from discussing European politics. Instead, the visitors were forced to listen to a boring discourse on Islam and its glories.

At tea time the Aga offered his guests whiskey and soda, which they refused, and Camel cigarettes which they accepted. They were served very strong Indian tea with twelve small cookies precisely arranged on a simple platter. Chase took two, although she was sure that only one was expected of her. When they left, their hosts thanked them profusely for coming to the villa. Chase admitted that, after she met the monarch's wife, her "manners toward the human race [would] always be better."

❡

The summer of 1953 was shrouded in sorrow. On August 7, the eve of his sixty-first birthday, Chase's cherished brother, Edward Everett, Jr., was killed in a plane crash. Edward, a prominent attorney and state senator, and William Tudor Gardiner, former Governor of Maine, were returning from their fortieth reunion at Bowdoin. Chase wrote Mildred that Edward's death was neither tragic or terrible, it was merciful and comforting compared with other misfortunes. The last time she saw him he remarked: "Well, if the Lord will only take me quickly out of this world while I am still of use, I'll be willing to overlook a few of His worst mistakes which I've always harbored against Him."

When she received the sad news, Chase phoned Duckett to say that "the family would like you to come to the funeral. But for mercy's sake don't go out and buy a black suit." Edward was devoted to Duckett, mainly because he still read Latin. Duckett accompanied her companion to Blue Hill, where Edward was buried next to his mother, who had worshipped him. Chase wrote Eleanor Lincoln that "eighteen Chases were all together, and I was proud of every one. . . . In fact, my whole large family deserves a 'Summa' for the way they have taken this . . . my pride in them is deeper even than my sorrow."

Chase received a spate of condolence letters, but she could not abide the outbursts of pity from most of the correspondents. She wrote Mathilde: "I'm so sick of gloom and ghastliness that I have an extra drink a day, though I don't much want it, but . . . it's a symbol of relative gaiety . . . I don't mind anything except outcries vs. life and I wouldn't mind those, if only people could curse like Job, but still be so alive in mind that you knew he couldn't be downed. The marvellous thing about old Job is that he's still triumphant though in the dust."

Shortly after Edward's death, Chase wrote *The White Gate: Adventures in the Imagination of a Child*. Published in 1954, it was an elongated version of "Recipe for a Magic Childhood," which appeared in the May 1951 issue of *Ladies Home Journal*.

In this engaging essay, Chase expressed her gratitude to her parents for their encouragement in discovering the magic of words long before they began their formal education.

"Recipe for a Magic Childhood" had appealed to so many readers that Chase's editors at Macmillan had urged her to write a story for juveniles about her childhood. Despite her initial hesitation to aim for a young audience, it was fascinating to recapture those vivid impressions, those glimpses of reality and wisdom, "like the flashing of fireflies in the darkness." Composed between November 1953 and March 1954, *The White Gate* was a best seller and elicited 1,600 letters of praise from admiring readers. With this memoir, Chase was acclaimed by discerning critics as a leading American literary stylist.

The White Gate marked Chase's debut with W.W. Norton. After twenty years, twelve books, and agonizing days of deliberation, she decided to seek a smaller publisher. She wrote Mathilde: "[Leaving Macmillan] was an awful wrench and I must say they were noble, though shocked and grieved. But they have grown into . . . an empire governed by almighty dollars . . . I don't want to make money. I want my books bound and printed beautifully and I want to deal with men who value books as books rather than money as money."

Chase and Storer Lunt, president of Norton, were kindred spirits. They both came from Maine, and their attachment to their native state forged a bond that lasted throughout Chase's life. When Marion Dodd, manager of the Hampshire Bookshop, invited Chase to a booksigning party, she asked Lunt to escort her. He accepted, stating that he did not want to be any place but there. He arrived in Northampton in time to have tea with Chase and, later, a hurried dinner at Rahar's. At the party Chase wore an understated eight-year-old dress which she said made her look like "an English schoolboy ready for matins." She looked tired and drawn, spoke in subdued tones to a receptive audience, signed hundreds of books, and went through the usual amenities expected of a celebrity. Of all the tributes she received that evening, the one that moved her the most was a note left on the autograph table by an unidentified student: "You don't only write about youth. You are youth itself, and you give us strength to go ahead."

CHAPTER SEVENTEEN

1954-1955

In 1955 Chase retired from the faculty of Smith College. The realization that she would be free from the daily stress of academic life was reassuring, but she was terrified at the thought that most of her life had gone. She wished she could be granted a second chance so that she might make a better job of it. At a farewell party given in her honor, the entire English faculty performed a clever charade based on her books. Though grateful for the attention showered upon her, she was sad to come to the end of this most vital aspect of her existence.

She wrote Mildred: "Once I am out of this maelstrom of meetings, candidates for jobs, farewell parties, etc., I mean to spend an hour a day on my Hebrew and to read every volume of my Loeb Classical Library." She was certain that her last year would be easy with no actual teaching involved. But she was wrong. She was asked to instruct twenty classes with two hundred students in each, to speak occasionally before the entire assembly, and to give readings in the library. She was expected to procure jobs for at least a dozen applicants, to chair a symposium on the modern novel, to donate her services to the town, to personally counsel at least one hundred discouraged and lovelorn girls, to select curtains for the infirmary, to plan a church school program, and to teach English to members of the Polish Men's Club.

Chase often reflected on the thousands of women she had taught and she did not remember actually loving any of them, "but I did love seeing their minds, trying to discern their thoughts, wondering what they loved and what they would hang on to through the years, longing to give them the thrill of evening grosbeaks, or of *Tom Jones,* or Rudolf Oth's *Idea of the Holy.*"

Chase's impact on her students was profound. Many of them relived their association with her long after graduation: "I can still see the large lecture room in Burton Hall with the sun pouring in the window," a former pupil recalled in the *Smith Alumnae Quarterly.* "Everything in the room is clear to me— with the exception of one small item—the clock. I can perform a little mental exercise by going through all the classrooms that figured in my college life and in every one of them I can plainly see the clock, but when I come to Burton 6, I have not the faintest notion of where the clock was located, or if there was one at all. What greater compliment could any teacher ask?"

A graduate student observed: "The classroom podium, where Chase sat behind the desk, was really the setting of a one man show! Her lectures were dramatic, often amusing, but always full of substance. . . . She used to say that there were two kinds of truth—literal truth and dramatic truth. She was often guilty of the latter."

Helen Randall, Chase's associate, labelled her a "hypothetical campus Scrooge." In an article in the August 1955 issue of the *Smith Alumnae Quarterly,* Randall noted: "She has no sense of propriety. Although a writer of her distinction should be at least to some degree a Bohemian, she is the outstanding housekeeper and cookie maker in Northampton, and instead of burning the midnight oil, she does a day's work right after dawn and telephones her colleagues when they should be up but are not. [In the college infirmary], no matter how severe her illness, she captivates staff and patients, sends off the usual steady flow of bright, enchanting letters which her countless friends preserve . . . she has perfectly caught the 'genius of the place' which is Smith College."

In January 1955 Elizabeth Cutter Morrow died. Morrow, class of 1896, was a propelling force in the development of the college. She was instrumental in increasing the college's en-

dowment fund, donating a dormitory in her name, and estab-
lishing a first-rate Alumnae Association. In 1939, after Neilson's retirement, she was asked to serve as Acting President, a
post which she held for a year. The 2,000 students who heard
her speak in John M. Greene Hall remembered her "small figure on the platform, the attractive and arched manner in
which she held her head, her friendly way of beginning her
morning talk."

Chase had an unusual relationship with Morrow's daughter,
Anne Morrow Lindbergh. Chase was Anne's role model; Anne
admired her prolific output and her ease of expression. Chase
was amazed at Anne's vivid imagination, her inventiveness, her
clarity and depth of compassion. When *Listen, The Wind* was
published, she wrote Anne: "Your book pleased me more than I
can tell you . . . My envy is lost in my praise . . . It has all the
characteristics of the best in fiction, of life made more real than
life ever is."

Although Anne was able to combine writing and marriage
successfully, Chase contended that the two careers were incom-
patible. In the 1950s the working woman was a rarity, often
censured by her peers as one who neglected her responsibility
as wife and mother. The emancipated female, personified in
Betty Friedan's bold and revolutionary book, *The Feminine
Mystique* (1963), would soon relinquish women from the bonds
of domesticity. Friedan referred to "the problem that has no
name stirring in the minds of many American women, the fact
that they were not satisfied even though they had all that society told them they needed for happiness: a home, a family, and
many women did not go into the workplace for fulfillment."

Among the luminaries Chase nurtured at Smith, who were
setting the pace for the modern feminist, was Sylvia Plath, class
of 1955. Chase and her colleague, the poet Elizabeth Drew,
were Plath's gurus; they exemplified the accomplishments that
could be achieved by distinguished, erudite women. Plath frequently went to Chase's home, where they discussed literature,

verse and the art of writing. Chase was convinced that Plath was destined to become a Muse of Poetry.

Before Chase visited Plath and her husband, Ted Hughes, she wrote Alison Grant, a former student: "I find that Sylvia's marriage to the Byronic Yorkshireman was quite favored by Newnham and that she is doing brilliant work and is very much liked and admired. I go to tea with them in their rather dreary digs this Friday. The rather dowdy, but kind Newnham dons . . . grant that Sylvia's husband suggests *Wuthering Heights* without the strength of Heathcliff; but they are inclined to give him points, and just now I am seeing his Pembroke tutor as to what manner of young man he really is. Quite likely I was wrong about his cold, gray eyes. He is at all events teaching in a preparatory school here, which information is hopeful."

Ted's Pembroke tutor told Chase that he was an able and industrious student, not a scholar (although he took high second in his exams), but a most interesting and promising young man. The teacher added that in his three years there, Ted was somewhat solitary, but always amenable, "unusual in quite the right sense." Plath's supervisors praised her work; they predicted that she would excel in the Tripos examinations, perhaps receiving the highest degree.

In January 1956 Chase wrote Robert Gorham Davis, chairman of Smith's English department, recommending Plath for an instructorship. She stated: "I have no powers whatsoever of judgment, but you may wish to examine them, for what my opinion is worth, and please don't hold it too highly. I feel that Sylvia would be a fine addition to our staff. I am sure she has remarkable gifts as a teacher as well as real promise as a writer. She is now twenty-five, mature and most attractive and most eager to teach. I have talked at length with her about her future. I think she would love to come to Smith though she is most modest about even the possibility of a one-year appointment."

In March 1957 Plath received official confirmation of her new post. But teaching intimidated her. She felt uncomfortable with her students, and the close scrutiny of her colleagues was unsettling. The following January, she resigned and moved to London with her husband.

Nineteen fifty-five may have signalled the end of Chase's teaching career, but she decided not to consider herself retired. She dealt with this emotional crisis in her usual way—she quickly found a substitute path and remained an active and popular lecturer for many years. Six hundred Mount Hermon boys never forgot the stirring speech she gave in Northfield in March. She recounted the tale of the cow in Ireland during the 1848 famine and how she owed her life to it. The boys listened attentively and gave her a standing ovation. As she drove away, the entire student body waved farewell. The headmaster, Howard Rubendall, wrote her: "I cannot recall an occasion since I have been at Mt. Hermon that equalled in delight and inspiration your talk to the boys . . . It is impossible for me to express our gratitude in terms that would measure our feeling."

Chase's lively discourse, "Imagination in the Old Testament," was the first of many on the subject and was the core material for her third Bible study, *Life and Language in the Old Testament*. Before the lecture, she admitted that she was "under a black cloud" and would not emerge from it until it was over. It was the first time in eight years that Chase addressed the entire Smith assembly and she dreaded it more than an "ordeal by fire." "I wouldn't mind the girls," she wrote Mildred, "but the cold eyes of my colleagues freeze me to the marrow and they will all be there." She thought her talk was extremely heretical since she presented the Old Testament not as the Law or about the Prophets or the Word of God, but as a triumph of the human imagination. Her book would be a completely unorthodox but thrilling examination of the Hebraic imagination, mostly in terms of language.

On February 1, 1955, Chase wrote the first 200 words of "Imagination in the Old Testament." The working title did not please Lunt, and Chase agreed; she thought it sounded more like a doctoral thesis. For a week she pondered over alternatives; the night before she sailed for England, another possibility flashed across her mind. *Life and Language in the Old Testament* was a perfect choice, for that was precisely what her book was about.

In mid-April Chase and Duckett boarded the *Mauretania*. Under the auspices of the Cunard Line they were given a sumptuous cabin which Chase thought resembled a bridal chamber. She craved luxury, especially when she did not have to pay for it. Desiring anonymity, they avoided socializing during the trip. Two of the dullest-looking passengers had copies of Chase's *The Bible and the Common Reader* in their overjewelled hands, but Chase did not notice anyone reading it.

When she arrived at the Garden House Hotel a cable from Lunt awaited her, stating that he preferred the title "The Glory of the Old Testament." She replied that she could not accept this, for it sounded more like a sermon given by Norman Vincent Peale. The Norton editors finally agreed on *Life and Language in the Old Testament*, and once the matter was resolved, Chase found that words "burst forth like springs in the desert."

On May 2 she wrote 1,000 words on the Hebraic sense of place. She labored six to eight hours daily and frequently worked past midnight. The following day, as a monstrous wind tore across the fens, forcing the blossoms from the pear tree and covering the ground with white petals, she completed the section on "Distinctive Qualities of the Hebrew Mind." She was approaching 20,000 words, the first third of the book. On May 18 she sent Lunt 6,000 words along with the table of contents.

When Lunt mailed the proposed book jacket, depicting the prophets, Chase told him that they looked like the "anthropomorphic idea of God in many or several distinctly unpleasant moods." "They strike an absolutely wrong note," she wrote. "This book deals with ideas and language and I think it's the best thing I have ever done. It hasn't the remotest connection with whatever those figures are meant to convey."

On June 2 Lunt informed Chase that the first section was "just elegant. I salute you." She wrote Mathilde that she considered "'Life and Language' at least a decent job, but I don't know. It surely is like nothing else in the Old Testament but therein may lie its failure . . . the ideas are curious, to say the least, and may well be untenable. I dare say the real scholars will stick knives in my ribs, but at least they can't say I don't know my Great Original whatever they may think of my conclusions."

Chase left Cambridge on May 19, leaving Duckett in England. After a perilous drive on rain-slicked roads to Southampton, she boarded the liner on June 4. She was aware of an impending stewards' strike, but was assured that the boat would depart on schedule. The following morning a disembarkation notice was posted and she was forced to find lodgings in the seedy Polygon Hotel. There was no available space on any ship for the returning vessels were fully booked.

It was an eerie feeling to be completely alone, unable to go anywhere due to a railway strike. Chase spent hours on her study in a strange, detached way. She wrote Lunt: "Only the Hebrews keep me going. I am ugly to look at, weary of travel bureaus, a bit dotty in my head." She became familiar with everything in the town, "every dog, child, shop, tired face." Frequent trips to the American Express office and the Counsel's office resulted in a reservation on the *Italia*, departing June 11 and reaching New York on June 20.

The day before she sailed was a memorable one. Chase was completely discouraged over the chapter on "Idea of a Journey in the Old Testament"; she was dejected in mind and spirit, tired of being delayed, sick of being alone, and almost physically ill from apprehension. She forced herself to take a two-mile walk to the Cow Herd Inn. As she strolled on, she was suddenly flooded with ideas and words. At the inn she ate her solitary steak dinner in a glow of rapture, loving her loneliness, wanting for nothing. Outside in the garden were Paul Scarlet roses in bloom, hanging from a trellis. She never forgot them, or her radiant walk back to the hotel.

Chase arrived in New York, tired but triumphant, with the entire manuscript in her briefcase. A week later she sent Lunt 188 pages, and he wrote her that they were "very, very good. I love the clear clocked use of your direct way with words. The book solidly conveys both a full knowledge and grasp of the subject, and your felicity of expression is in itself a leaf out of the subject matter." The book was completed on July 8, the day before she left for Windswept.

The month spent at Windswept was dismal. Chase decided she must sell the house since it was too expensive to maintain and its very remoteness proved to be a problem when she was ill with pleurisy. By the time it was ready for the Pearls, the new occupants, she was so exhausted that she could not summon up a tear. She bought new window shades, made twelve pairs of curtains, washed and rebound every blanket, and left every window gleaming. The night before she left, she noted in her journal: "Tonight I shall sit in the white candle light for the last time. And yet I feel nothing but an odd relief. I shall pull this curtain very quickly over these sixteen years."

Along with the house keys, Chase left the Pearls a brief note: "Just now, I do not think I shall ever return here. . . . I rather like to end the chapters of my life summarily. Still, one never knows one's mind. This quite cheerful and happy statement means only one thing: that I do not wish you ever to think of me or any of my former possessions with the least degree of [sentiment]. They are all yours to do with as you wish. I am more pleased than I can say that you are having this house, this shoreline, these mornings and evenings. They have all made my New Jerusalem for sixteen years, and will, in an odd way, continue to do so. I leave without a shadow of regret—only vast gratitude."

Back in Northampton, Chase tried to forget Windswept, but nearly every night she dreamed she was there, watching the stars and the dramatic contours of Mount Cadillac. "I'm not denying it was a wrench," she wrote Mathilde, "but in an odd way I seem to possess it all in some kind of invulnerable fastness. I find myself living there hour by hour, maybe in the same sort of way St. John lived when, chained in Patmos in the quarries, he had to transform his Judean hills, for which he was so homesick, into his New Jerusalem."

CHAPTER EIGHTEEN

1956-1957

A portrait of Chase, commissioned by Helen and Robbins Milbank, was unveiled in April 1957 in the Smith College library's Browsing Room. Chase warned her friends that they would be wasting their money transposing her to canvas for she thought she was unphotogenic. It was, she said, "an odd collection of Hollywood and Heaven," but conceded that her gray suit and white blouse were effectively drawn.

That year Chase began work on *The Edge of Darkness*. She escaped to England to finish it, for she could not concentrate on it in Northampton or anywhere else in this country. She told Lunt that she would return with the completed manuscript in her suitcase and stated emphatically that she did not want it cut since it was bare enough with every word counting. It was a presentation of ten people, singly or in pairs, in which the untold stories were more significant than the told, and even more moving. She added that it was the sort of thing in which what is not said was far more important than what is stated. She did not imply that it was vague or merely symbolic, for the novel was most accurate and realistic. She wanted the book to be open and spacious, with the plot merely suggested in the lives of the leading characters. When she read proof she realized how many of these individual struggles there were and she purposely partially narrated them so that the action would not intrude upon the central meaning.

By March 1 the novel neared its end; the final section was rewritten at least six times before Chase was satisfied with it. She wrote Lunt: "At least the isolated places on the Maine coast have never been so thoroughly done. And I can't help thinking the characters have real appeal and not a little drama—also truth." She told Katie Barnard, Lunt's editorial assistant, that "those days and weeks spent not only on the edge of darkness, but in actual darkness, took a lot out of me." The Norton publishers seemed very keen about it, but Chase feared it might be dull reading for it was about simple, good and obscure individuals.

Chase was not sure whether her "inconsequential and probably mediocre" book was good or not; she wrote Mathilde: "I have slaved over it for nine weeks of despair, darkness, loneliness, indecision. Why anyone voluntarily enters this long, dark tunnel of discouragement, indecision and even despair, with no help but Roget and God, I would not know . . . I do know I'll never do it again."

An eminent contemporary English author once described the discontent of all writers as "the long despair of doing nothing well." This is an apt assessment of what most novelists feel as they labor ceaselessly over their work. In 1929 when Chase met Willa Cather, Cather was writing *Shadows on the Rock*. Cather said: "I wrote one good sentence this morning. I mean *really* good, but I realize far too well that it can't redeem my general sense of failure . . . 'Shadows' mean more to me than mere substance. It won't have a trace of what people call movement or surprise. It will just have people and a lot of things." Chase knew exactly what she meant, for she was just the same.

Cather was at her best when she talked about writing, preferably the works of others rather than her own. Chase recalled her idea of design and pattern as opposed to situation and plot. "I can't write plots," Cather admitted, "I don't see life in terms of action. Persons like me who have to see it in terms of thought and imagery would best keep away from plots. It's design they want, not conflict, not episodes which get tangled up with other episodes." Her exquisite book *My Antonia* is held together by design—its pattern, the recurring red, waving grass appears again and again in her simple, spare pages. *Shadows on the Rock* is given form by the old French candlesticks, a silver cup, the glass fruit of Count Frontenac, the sea-battered ships sailing up the St. Lawrence. When Chase asked Cather the secret of her success, the modest author answered: "Oh, just as usual—by things which mean something—like a child's mug can."

At the time of their first encounter, Cather was in her mid-fifties, fourteen years older than Chase. She was a handsome woman, almost beautiful, of average height and distinctly over-weight. She had certain arresting features which one never forgot. Her complexion was clear and smooth, Chase recalled, "not like Dresden china but rather like the outside of any well-tempered plate just off a white color, perhaps like cream. Her face was startling in its absence of lines. Her mouth was gener-ous and good-humored. Her eyes were her most remarkable fea-ture, long rather than round eyes and of a clear blue, neither dark nor light. Her gaze was direct and open. She always looked directly at one with an expression of deepest interest . . . she was not a person who craved for or sought human relations. The people she cared for were not those whom she met, but rather those whom she created . . . "

Like Cather, Chase was aware of the rigors of writing. She described the author's sense of failure as the "painful knowledge that we can never do what we long to do; this unwilling recog-nition that a character hasn't really come to life, that a scene is overdone or underdone, lacks strength and conviction; this irritating, or perhaps better, heartbreaking admission that words might have been more happily chosen; this sudden real-ization that some dramatic or appealing detail has been over-looked, has come to mind too late . . . Only 'the long despair' remains . . . We may . . . have had the courage to write our books; yet we lack the fortitude to read them ourselves . . . "

The actual writing of *The Edge of Darkness* took only nine weeks, but it was in Chase's mind for five years. It was her favorite among all her works, and she considered it her most comprehensive book, the finest in terms of form and language. Yet she dreaded its appearance: "people will see what I really am—something which God has a right to know. I don't suppose anyone can ever know how one suffers from this disclosure of oneself, but I'm willing to die rather than endure these next few months." When she sent the Milbanks advance copy, she advised them not to be overly enthusiastic: "Don't expect to be excited! You will discover no Mr. Motos or Hercule Poirots or Lord Peter Whimseys. You will *not* learn the power of positive thinking or how to win friends and influence people. There are no bedroom scenes . . . after the prescribed pattern, about which I am not only ignorant, and in which I have little or no interest. But on a rainy evening you may enjoy reading this quiet, inconsequential thing. Don't hasten to do so!"

The Norton editors were deeply impressed. Lunt said that it was "superb," but he suggested that it needed extensive editing. When he and Katie Barnard began to change certain words and delete significant passages, Chase was upset. In the editing process, much of the original meaning, the depth, and tenderness of expression, were ruthlessly slashed. As a perfectionist, she could not tolerate even one inaccurate word.

Chase wrote Barnard a candid letter concerning unwarranted editing: "I rather like my job. I really think it's a nice book and a far better one because of the pages you wanted left out. Also to read it does something to my often waning faith in miracles or mysteries. I just can't believe I wrote it; in fact, I haven't the least tangible memory of those days in Cambridge when I labored on. All the words and scenes seem completely unfamiliar to me now—which goes to prove beyond the shadow of a doubt that some strange presence was in that room at the Garden House, quietly dictating to me. In other words, it's not my work."

Chase had trepidations about her novels that focused on Maine since she feared she might not accord her native state its rightful recognition. *Mary Peters*, *Silas Crockett*, and *The Edge of Darkness* are based securely on Maine history and Maine life; their chief aim is the portrayal of authentic villages and their inhabitants. *The Edge of Darkness* had a title long before it was written. That lovely phrase is used in eastern Maine to describe twilight, the end of day, when the sky holds a long, steady glow of light. It is the story of a small coast village sadly changed from its former days. Were it not for Sarah Holt, whose death forms and frames the novel, its dwellers might have been unaware that their village was once an integral part of the sea-faring world. Sarah's past is a touchstone, it unites the disparate lives of the cove dwellers who mourn her passing.

The format differs radically from the author's usual style. Elizabeth Drew told Chase that "Edge" had no form whatso-ever, but Chase contended that Drew was unfamiliar with her technique. She planned it methodically so that each section would characterize the dead woman. It is composed throughout on the principle of understatement, on the desire to awaken the reader's mind to thoughts and perceptions never allowed to appear on the pages. Each chapter in the main section is a story in itself, one of accident, fear or tragedy, of love and wisdom, of thwarted hopes and desires, of wrong and its resultant miseries. The characters' lives are touched and transformed by Sarah's death as they are slowly enveloped in a gathering sense of loss.

Several critics maintained that the book was really a series of vignettes, like Jewett's *The Country of the Pointed Firs*, where the author achieves a structure independent of plot. However, the interconnected chapters indicate a distinct pattern of sev-eral narratives radiating like spokes from the central persona of Sarah Holt. Lucy Norton and Sarah, two equally important fig-ures, originated from Chase's admiration of Jewett's method in *The Country of the Pointed Firs*. Both books are accounts of remote coastal hamlets; they depict the seedy and the pathetic as well as the vibrant and heartening aspects of Maine coast life.

The Edge of Darkness generated 35,000 sales before its publication on October 28, 1957. Chase knew that she was "clearly in for all the things I hate the most—confusion, so-called success, autograph seekers and no beautiful, free hour in which to watch a yellow leaf drift down." When Lunt sent her a substantial check, she told him that she was "thrilled for the Maine girl who earned it all by herself. For even the most perfect of publishers can't sell poor or mediocre wares . . . thank you for taking the risk and the chance."

Paul Jordan-Smith, literary editor of the *Los Angeles Times*, observed: "It is rare in this decade to meet a novelist who can see life in the round; who is able to understand, at all levels of life, the conflict between good and evil; who is possessed by the integrity to present her vision of life fully and clearly, and the grace to do it in terms of beauty and distinction."

Sterling North read the manuscript in one long sitting. He wrote Lunt: "Mary has lost none of her magic. She chose a very difficult form but she brought it off with great skill. . . . Not since Sarah Orne Jewett have we had a better look at Maine." Lunt agreed, he said the novel was truly "the very bone and marrow of the Maine coast."

Chase and North had become friends in 1942 when he came to her aid after her fall in Chicago's Drake Hotel. Although the articles editor of the *Chicago Daily News* was nearly two decades younger than Chase, he had followed her career closely. For a quarter of a century he was proud to express his delight in her books. In his review of *Mary Peters* he had noted that "this novel is as rich a harvest as any New England fisherman ever brought in from the Banks of Newfoundland, as rich as any basket of apples from a New England orchard." In 1944 he wrote a glowing tribute to *The Bible and the Common Reader,* which he returned to constantly for comfort and strength.

The Chase–North correspondence, initiated in 1957 and continuing until 1965, constitutes a lively, informative and insightful series of letters. In his multifaceted profession as writer, editor and critic, North was subjected to a plethora of mail. His sole consolation was his congenial communication with Chase; he regarded her as the most distinguished of his authors.

In August 1957 North wrote Chase suggesting that she might be willing to donate her talents to a series aimed at the instruction of young Americans. He wanted a book that had adventure and romance, stressing courage and character in the face of adversity, a tale of loyal captains' wives who followed their mates to the end of the earth and of those who remained at home.

Sailing the Seven Seas was fun to write since Chase experienced none of the "pain and peril" which *The Edge of Darkness* exacted. She felt a bit proud of herself for having completed two books in her seventieth year, given, according to the psalmist, "only to labour and to sorrow." After he read it, North wrote her that "Seven Seas" was thoughtful, poetic and stately. Chase thanked him for his spirited reception: "That knowledge adds a great many cubits to my stature . . . I cherish your words, saying them over at night when I wake to hear the mighty winds straight over these fens from Siberia . . . This fen country has its charms. I never thought I'd come to love it better than I love Cornwall; but after months and even years here, I think I do. The sky is so close, the streams so quiet, the ricks so much a part of the earth."

Chase wrote three books for the North Star series: *Sailing the Seven Seas, Donald McKay and the Clipper Ships,* and *The Fishing Fleets of New England.* Although "Seven Seas" was the most popular in terms of sales, Chase's favorite was "Donald McKay," for the subject matter lay at the core of her lifelong interest in Maine's maritime history.

CHAPTER NINETEEN

The Dark Night of the Soul
1958-1960

By February 1958 *The Edge of Darkness* was in its fifth printing, with 43,000 copies sold. Norton offered Omnibook World
Wide Syndicate the rights to a condensed version which appeared in all member newspapers on the weekend of May 10-
11. As further evidence of her triumph, Chase was awarded an
annual book award. This distinction would have a marked
effect on the number of school library purchases of the novel
and would ensure the long, long life predicted by the publishers.

During the summer of 1958 Chase worked on an introduction to Fielding's *Joseph Andrews*, one of her favorite eighteenth-century novels. She promised Lunt that she would complete it by early fall before she sailed for England. But this trip
was cancelled due to unforeseen circumstances: in her seventy-
first year Chase was confronted with a devastating illness that
altered the course of her life.

On September 5, 1958, during a routine physical, Dr.
Averill detected a mass in Chase's right breast. Five days later
at Massachusetts General Hospital, Dr. Richard Sweet performed a radical mastectomy and removed a malignant growth
five inches long. He also excised all suspicious glands and the
area surrounding the nodule. Chase had serious cardiac compli-
cations and hovered near death for several days. The post-operative trauma and her initial inability to rally caused considerable apprehension. However, by September 20 she began to
show slight signs of improvement. That morning she called
Duckett to say that she had slept well and was wearing earrings

again. Duckett marvelled at her spirits; she wrote friends that "Mary rises from the ashes persistently and indomitably."

When Sterling North was informed of Chase's condition, he sent Duckett a note, asking her not to disclose the contents if she thought it was too solemn. Duckett replied: "The reaction to the strain of her illness is leaving her really content to avoid all exertion of mind and our great endeavor is to keep her from worrying or concentrating on any problem." She added that the beautiful editions of *Sailing the Seven Seas* made her companion "happy beyond words—and far more so because of all those concerned in its making . . . when she lovingly looked it through I was able to read to her from her own book. Mary sings your praises all the time—she says you are just you—no one in the writing world like you." North wrote Chase: "What a wonderful old sea-going captain you are, to rally after such a terrible operation. What currently worries me is that you are even thinking of working on the last 5,000 words of 'Seven Seas.' I would never forgive myself if anything so postponable as the manuscript would slow your recovery . . . just get well and you will be doing all of us the biggest favor. I have the greatest faith that you will live and live and live, and write great books for another couple of decades."

Chase's chief anxiety those first few days was the amount of blood transfusions required. She wrote North that never in her life had she come so close to "the Lord, since I emulate Him some sixteen hours a day by being wrapped in swaddling clothes and lying in a manger. I must say I'm a bit sick of this tiresome episode and in my darker moments wonder whether it's worth what it is costing, not only in literal thousands of dollars, but in thousands of other emotional prices, hard to assess, but terribly real." The medical staff thought Chase was far more interesting than the Wall Street tycoons convalescing in adjacent rooms. They were amazed at her resiliency and perseverance. Though concerned about her physical condition, she was sustained by an abiding faith. She wrote Mathilde:

"God knows I haven't learned much in this life . . . but if I even glimpsed a jot, it is that to fuss and fume after reasons is an horrendous and terribly depressing waste of time."

Chase completed "Donald McKay" in the hospital. She urged North to give her his honest opinion, not to be gentle because "a few waves and billows have washed over me. I'm sure there's smooth sailing ahead and I want a good book." He told her that she should be very proud of herself to have accomplished this task: "Just as in golf, polo and horse racing they place added burdens, restrictions or conditions upon the best performers, making winning more difficult, you have asked yourself to carry extra impedimenta. And here you are, victorious despite all."

North sent Chase some early reviews of "Seven Seas" while she was recuperating. The first was a rave notice from the not always complimentary Virginia Kirkus who devoted an entire page to the North Star series. She commended the serious, intelligent and beautifully printed nature of the series and noted that "Seven Seas" was "Splendid . . . A Maine background and forebears who sailed the seven seas combine to equip this author superbly for a book which one twelve-year-old characterized as 'neat.' . . . This emerges as an intimate, personal picture of a way of life when sailing ships . . . made history for this country."

Chase's recovery was prolonged due to the slow healing of the incision. The surgeon grafted tissue from her leg to her right breast. She had another opening through her rib cage where a drainage tube was inserted. The pain was severe, but it was nothing compared to the "degrading invasions of places that belong to oneself . . . the really awful intrusions, even the putting out of one's spirits, reducing it to a pile of gray ashes which can't . . . be fanned to glow again. There is seemingly nothing left of me that alien minds can't look upon . . . everything is merely outward and visible—there is nothing of the inward and spiritual left in me!"

Chase was discharged in late October. For the next 119 days she was supervised by Helen Brown, a capable but exasperating nurse, who had attended her during the night shift. She described her as a combination of "Saint, Gorgon, and the Rock of Ages. She is paid for eight hours, labors sixteen, watches twenty-four. She is the soul of goodness, virtue, mercy, kindness—and I could brain her with the fire tongs a dozen times a day!"

The stark realization that she had cancer resulted in a sense of bitterness and anger. The only thing that sustained her was her latest book. In *The Lovely Ambition* she fashioned a world so real that she actually lived in it for eighteen months. The novel, which she wrote for "cash, for self-defense, for fun," is the story of John Tillyard, a Wesleyan parson, who emigrated to America with his family in the early 1900s. The parson was her ideal of the right sort of person. She implied that her father embraced many of his ideals, despite "some bitter ironies."

The novel was the only book Chase wrote in first-person narrative. She wrote Sterling North that by early March it had reached the stage where "its people move themselves about and tell me what they are like. It's laid half in Suffolk, half in Maine. I have days when I think it's good, other days when only adventure keeps me from throwing it in the trash can . . . I know it's fairly well written, but whether it has any other value, I wonder . . . I can't bear to destroy it, for it has quite literally hauled me through days of frightening depression and I'm grateful to it."

Chase lived with a book until it was ready to be put on paper. She never made an outline, except in her head; then she transcribed it in a tablet from the five and dime. She usually wrote between 1,000 and 2,000 words a day, mostly during the morning hours. There was little revision required, for she was always very sure of what she wanted to say. She wrote "just as I cook or polish silver—most methodically and carefully. A book to me is just a job to be done as well as I can do it. I rarely make false starts or any other trials. I may and do live in it for weeks or months or years until it's ready to be set down on paper. Then I set them down and except for most minor changes, I leave it as it is. I have a way of going around the house saying sentences over and over until they sound ready for paper, then I just set them down and leave them."

Chase had a superstitious side, and one of her fixations was marble. In her bedroom at Windswept was a piece of marble that had been there for fourteen years. When she was not smoking, she held the stone in her left hand. It inspired her when she was writing *Windswept* and *The Bible and the Common Reader*. In the summer of 1944, when there were no electric lights except from a nearby farmhouse and never any at night, she penned the last chapter on Job and the section on St. Paul by two candles, one at her right shoulder, the other at her left. She was certain that the blue artifact, which captured and diffused the early morning light, made possible the completion of these works.

Chase wrote the first chapter of *The Lovely Ambition* six times before she was partially satisfied. When she sent it to Lunt he wrote her that he thought the working title, "A Land of Promise," a "natural and comfortable and solidly appropriate Mary Ellen Chase title." Chase disagreed, for the novel was basically the tale of a family, and she wanted to imply that from the start. At her request, the name was changed to *The Lovely Ambition*. She told Katherine Barnard that she considered it the best writing she had ever done, but if Barnard ranked it a D-, she had her permission to toss it in the wastebasket.

Chase became very independent with this novel. She had learned a lot about unnecessary editing when she wrote *The Edge of Darkness*. She wrote Mathilde: "I've had the experience in the past . . . [editors] telling me what they want and then deciding that they don't want it . . . Besides I have a far higher conception of what readers want or at least will take if we only accord them some respect. When the book was done . . . I sent it to Norton with a letter saying that they could take it or leave it precisely as it was, that I wouldn't change a page or even a paragraph, that it was the best thing I could do . . . I knew I had no energy or willingness to change a sentence. I'm sure the office was filled with consternation and very likely fury, but they meekly said 'OK, as it is,' and of course I shall probably have to bear the consequences."

Unlike *The Edge of Darkness*, which commemorates an honorable woman's death, *The Lovely Ambition* is an affirmation of the sheer joy of life. It is a portrait gallery, a study primarily of John Tillyard, an account of all he loves and believes. The Wesleyan parson is a virtuous man who lives in a fantasy world and believes that "life is better than it is, or can be made better if everyone does his best to make it so." Chase records the family history for fifty years; the narrator, reflecting on this period and on "tyranny and cruelty and sin which might have lessened even my father's lovely ambitions and tenacious faith," acknowledges that he belonged to another time, but we do believe that in that time he lived. He had great faith in this country: "There's something in America that I can't find anywhere else, at least not to the same extent. I think it's a kind of respect for the human mind, for what it can and must become. Perhaps hope describes it better than any other word . . . I hope America . . . won't forget what she really has meant and can mean to countless millions of people everywhere in the world."

The novel is a search for a way of life that is balanced, serene, and rational in a world of loss. Chase stresses the importance of family strength in healing wounds of disruption. In her own words: "It is a story for those who still believe that in the character of families lies our chief hope or despair, for the redemption of this erring, perplexed and overburdened world."

The Lovely Ambition was completed on November 11, 1959. By the summer, sales reached 40,000, as well as two and a quarter million copies in the *Reader's Digest* Condensed Book Club version. It also appeared in two installments in the *Philadelphia Sunday Bulletin* on July 10 and July 23, 1960. Its rivals on the best seller list of November 27, 1960 were Allen Drury's *Advise and Consent*, James Michener's *Hawaii*, and Harper Lee's *To Kill a Mockingbird*. Chase's work was in seventh place for the twenty-second consecutive week; a month later it was fourth.

North observed that it was a rich, readable and rewarding novel. He knew that Chase had spent many seasons in England, but was amazed at her keen perception of Suffolk, for the lambing meadows, the streams, the market towns: "You give us the feel of the region as thoroughly as Mary Webb captures her native Shropshire. Your whole novel has texture, like a good English tweed . . . the cloth wears as well when you import it to your own Maine. . . . " Lunt commented: "I say that this book is very good. I say I like it. We shall make it our leading book on our Norton spring list and go after it hammer and tong . . . I trust that we can reach markets beyond your ever loyal and devoted readers."

By Christmas 1960 Chase had received over one thousand letters; one reader wrote that she "should have been called Beatrice, though I don't suppose there was any way for your parents to know that you would be leading out of Paradise Pond into fields that must be paradises, discovered or regained by thousands." She also acquired twenty pounds of cheese, four poinsettias, six fruit cakes, two Christmas puddings, two cartons of grapefruit, four boxes of Rose Marie chocolates, two hand-embroidered sheets, six assorted handkerchiefs, one cyclamen plant, three boxes of fragrant soaps, and a dozen camellias.

Chase wrote Mildred Hillhouse that she was not "a bit swelled about that wretched book." She was sure she would never have the courage to write another novel, for *The Lovely Ambition* had been costly in many respects: "Don't ever envy a best selling author whether or not (and I do not) he deserves it. I am writing a book on the Psalms, but with the results of this recent one messing up my life, I can't say that my progress is marked, or at the moment, my enthusiasm."

In January 1961 Katie Barnard reported on the adventures of *The Lovely Ambition*, which had been on the best-seller list for eight months: *Reader's Digest*, Omnibook Syndicate; British and other foreign editions including German and Spanish; an award from the Independent Schools Education Board as one of the ten best books of the year for the pre-college reader, and an invitation to be guest of honor at the *New York Herald Tribune* American Bookseller's Association Book and Author Luncheon in February 1961.

V.

The Nineteen Sixties

CHAPTER TWENTY

The Hope and The Dream

On February 20, 1961, Chase delivered the keynote speech at the Waldorf Astoria. The annual Book and Author Luncheon, attended by 1200, was the largest group she had ever addressed. She accepted the invitation to please Storer Lunt, who thought her presence would encourage sales of *The Lovely Ambition*, for Irita Van Doren who had asked her to speak, and for the chance to see Noel Coward again. She had first met him in 1957 on a trans-Atlantic crossing; she recalled that he was often slightly inebriated on the voyage. Coward had been invited to talk along with the less appealing author Morris West, whose controversial book, *The Devil's Advocate*, had recently been published.

Chase approached the rostrum with her customary air of bravado, though she later admitted that she was "scared to death." Her topic was the lack of majestic themes and gallant characters in current fiction. She noted that she had something in common with the other participants: they had all written novels and knew how demanding that profession could be. She thought that Coward and West, like most men, looked rather skeptically upon teachers, "especially older ones like me . . . but still on the whole they're harmless and many of them are rather nice."

Chase claimed that a novel was not basically a story, but an evaluation of life. The story was merely a means to an end, the vehicle which conveyed the author's belief on the meaning of life. She mentioned that *The Lovely Ambition* had a very frail plot; the two factors that established it were Stephen Spender's poem and the symbolic import of the doll's shoe that she had unearthed in the abbey ruins at Bury St. Edmunds.

The thrust of her message was that noble themes and heroic characters had virtually disappeared from the modern novel. The great, struggling figures such as George Apley, Cash McCall, or even Job, were created when writers believed that man could be triumphant, if not over his fate, over his spirit. She attributed this lack of fortitude to the new wave of psychotherapy. She claimed that therapists interfered with the mysteries of the human persona and the yearnings of the soul by declaring that man's fate is preordained, determined by inheritance, or by emotional events in his childhood. She concluded by observing that "perhaps our present day fiction will give us little or nothing until we return to the old verities of the human spirit, until we refuse to allow the psychologists to convince us that man is irretrievably caught by the snares of his past."

Her talk was acknowledged with an enthusiastic round of applause and a surge of admirers rushing to the platform to purchase her books. The day was especially memorable because of Coward's reaction. He embraced her, saying that he wished he could write a play in which she would have the leading role. He praised her well-modulated voice and said her delivery was "perfection." Chase was overcome by this unexpected display of affection; she spent the rest of the day recovering in her hotel.

In late July Bowdoin College honored Chase at a special Convocation Day. Eight hundred people attended, including

Smith alumnae and distinguished Maine residents. The afternoon was unbearably hot; Chase felt sick every moment. She wrote Mathilde that she "felt so awful all those days that I don't see how I made a speech. . . . I thought the speech C- at best, but seemingly it wasn't too bad, though I recall precisely nothing about it."

Chase was introduced by President Coles, and she listened politely to his laudatory remarks. She spoke about her new book on the Psalms, although she did not mention it by name. Bela Norton, Bowdoin's vice-president, noted that the occasion was a distinct success: "Everything went off very smoothly and Miss Chase made a most interesting appearance. She moved around the stage and spoke in very soft tones so that there was some difficulty in hearing. However, she . . . literally had the audience in the palm of her hand. . . . She spoke about an hour which was a bit on the longish side . . . but she was so absorbed in her subject and it was so good that it really didn't bother. . . . All in all it was a first rate convocation and she keeps the standard high." Chase was offered a substantial honorarium, but kept only enough to cover her expenses, donating the remainder to Bowdoin's Alumni Fund.

Chase completed her fourth Bible study, *The Psalms for the Common Reader* in November 1961. She considered that it was "only a simple primer, though it took three years of study." She rated it a B+ for a "rather decent job" since she succeeded in elucidating the Psalms, which she considered a "mess in the form the Bible gives them." In the *New York Times* Book Review, Liston Pope noted: "This book is not the standard type of scientific or historical analysis most characteristic of Biblical scholarship. . . . Its uniqueness lies precisely in its combination of academic accuracy, literary insight and felicity. . . . Here the professor of English literature and the student of Hebrew are integrated with most happy results." Virginia Corwin, chairman of Smith's department of religion, told Chase the book was outstanding; she urged her to write another on the prophets.

Sterling North wrote Chase: "I am under a spell. Let this be your first critical acclaim. I love the Psalms for the common reader. I wish I had a column and twenty-five syndicated outlets. I would really do a tender and appreciative review of this book." He added that it was "the most moving, the most scholarly, the most poetic and the most readable book ever written on the Psalms."

The first printing generated 17,500 copies. On April 11, 1962, there was a second printing of 5,000, the Book Club Guild sold 4,000, a total exceeding 20,000. By the end of the month Norton's two leaders in sales were the historian, Barbara Ward, and Chase; Lunt was certain that Chase would ultimately surpass Ward and would continue to prevail for many years.

Louis Untermeyer, an editor at Crowell Collier, was so impressed that he asked Chase to contribute to an unusual series of books aimed at beginning readers, *Modern Masters Books for Children*. He offered a $2,000 advance for a four- to ten-page article. After reading the essay he wrote her: "Every child will read it with delight. My wife and I forgot our own ages as we went through it." Untermeyer sent the manuscript to Harlan Quist, editor of the firm's juvenile department. It was subsequently printed in *Show*, a magazine unknown to Chase.

To commemorate her seventy-fifth birthday, the March 1962 issue of the *Colby Library Quarterly* was devoted entirely to Chase. Duckett composed a tender portrait of her companion. She described her as a warm and vital woman who never tried to impress anyone with her erudition: "My friend does not try to collect knowledge, as many of us do. . . . She absorbs it, almost unconsciously, and it is all there, ready for its own day and hour."

Between September 1961 and July 1962 Chase was hospitalized in six different medical centers, five in Boston and one in Northampton. Despite a long siege of phlebitis, she felt more fortunate than most of her fellow men. To add to her discomfort, she had arthritis in her right hand and arm. That summer she was forbidden to take any long drives, so she stayed home with a "Polish pearl of great price in the kitchen." This meticulous housekeeper told Chase that she had the cleanest house in the country.

In her seventh decade Chase's outlook on life changed. She became more reclusive, shunned most social engagements and lost some of her faith in mankind. On a voyage to England she was appalled at the pretentiousness of the American passengers. "I needed the hope and the dream," she wrote the Milbanks. "After fifty years of faith in 'the people,' I have begun to wonder. And the *Queen Elizabeth* sadly increased the wonder and the depression. The *Caronia* in Southampton, after a Mediterranean cruise, spewed into our homecoming midst 400 of the most deplorable Americans . . . dripping with mink, fat, dull, and too stupid for any words of mine to characterize . . . these 400 . . . were so intolerable that any hope of civilization became almost non-existent."

In late 1962 Chase composed her fifth and final Bible study, *The Prophets for the Common Reader*. She admitted that it was harder to write than "Psalms," for her concentrative powers were diminishing and she could not work the long hours she had before. Lunt loved the book. He told Chase that the prophets "come alive as real and contemporary personalities, as though you actually knew them. It is a pleasure to read so clear, so well organized and beautifully written a manuscript. You continue to delight and surprise. I am greatly indebted to you. It is just grand to have so fine a book ahead. It adds lustre to our imprint. This is publishing at its best. My eternal thanks and gratitude are yours."

North wrote Chase: "Two such brilliant women under one roof. You do not need the prophets to add to your combined wisdom." He was aware that the prophets were "a problem and that you could not make them attractive without a great deal of research, interpretation and talented writing . . . Like all your books it will be something to treasure."

North urged Chase to write a fourth book for the North

Star series. He thought that Captain John Smith would be a fascinating subject, for his story was steeped in folklore, especially regarding his fabled romance with Pocahontas. This topic did not appeal to Chase, but she was willing to do almost anything for her friend. North then suggested a suspenseful tale of lighthouses along the Atlantic coast, a factual account dating from the time of the oldest ediface, Pharos of Alexandria, the Roman lights and the great Eddystone light, to the ledges of Maine and Tillamook. The material was inexhaustible, especially around the Cape Hatteras area where hundreds of ships were lost when the Gulf Stream collided with the southward flowing current.

The Story of Lighthouses had an eventful publication history. North thought it surpassed "Donald McKay" and "Fishing Fleets" and equal to "Seven Seas," but he had reservations about the context. Although he could not find any structural problems in the opening sections, he was disappointed in the fifth chapter, since there was a great deal of repetition which lessened the overall impact. He wrote Austin Olney, Norton's art director: "The book picks up in Chapter Six . . . and becomes perfectly delightful in the last three chapters . . . this prose has the classic simplicity which makes Mary, at her best, one of our great stylists. . . . As usual with Mary's copy, I think we should be quite restrained and appreciative. She surely works hard for our series."

Olney considered that "Lighthouses" would be more suitable as a Houghton Mifflin juvenile selection. He contended that there was an ethical matter involved, since Chase was under contract to Norton. North disagreed: if it was appropriate for Houghton Mifflin, why not include it in the North Star series? He was sure that he could sell the manuscript almost anywhere; there were at least seven publishers who wanted Chase to sign a contract immediately. "But I won't," he wrote Olney, "since I trust you implicitly to protect her, to protect yourself, to protect me and to protect the series."

Ten days later Olney wrote George Brockway at Norton what he thought of "Lighthouses": it was a "nice piece of work filled with the charm of Chase's personality and one that we would very much like to publish. North Star books deal entirely with themes from American history and the present manuscript concerns itself to a large degree with a European and Old World background. . . . Although all this material is entirely appropriate to the book, we feel that we cannot in all conscience include it in the series."

At this time Chase was editing Jewett's stories for Norton; she also had a further commitment to Coward McCann for a piece on the forty-eight states, and another to E.P. Dutton for an account of her teaching experiences. Publication of *The Story of Lighthouses* was delayed until 1965 when it was issued by Norton.

CHAPTER TWENTY-ONE

Last Years
1962-1973

During the last eight years of her literary life, Chase was in great demand as a writer, but she was always prudent in her choice of topics. She never compromised her lofty style for monetary reasons. She did not like self-appraisals or confessionals, but elected to highlight one fundamental virtue or value. She avoided reprints, preferring to submit something fresh and new. She had her share of rejections: in 1958 she wrote a piece on the Aga Khan for Frank Lewis, deputy editor of *Parade* magazine. Edith Haggard, who kept a sharp eye on suitable markets for Chase, liked the story, but Lewis was unimpressed. A few months later Chase wrote a sentimental tale, "I'll Always Remember," for the same journal. Lewis told Haggard that he would have to revise it to meet *Parade*'s specifications, but the editor-in-chief did not think it would appeal to his readership.

Chase refused assignments whose topics were distasteful. Richard Kaplan, editor of *Coronet*, requested an article entitled "What Men Should Know About Women," based on her long experience as professor and advisor of the lovelorn at Smith. He was sure that she had mentally catalogued the blunders some men make in their approach to the opposite sex. Chase was appalled; she said she could not comply with this suggestion: "I don't know enough. I just don't want to. It just isn't possible, at least for me, to do anything of this sort with any dignity at all. I just can't stick this confessional sort of thing. I'd die of embarrassment. I'm a stodgy old professor who doesn't want to earn money—at least not at this price."

In February 1959 Chase received a letter from Catherine Fennelly, editor of *Galaxy*, an attractive new magazine published by Old Sturbridge Village, asking her to write on anything she chose. Chase kept postponing the assignment, first because of ill health, then due to the pressure of finishing *The Lovely Ambition*, and once again because she wanted to contribute something original. Eventually, she sent her a charming essay, "Land Sakes Alive!" which appeared in the periodical's April 1960 issue. When Fennelly sent a check for $200, Chase was bewildered for she had made it clear that she did not want any compensation. "Have you in Sturbridge gone quite mad?" she wrote Fennelly. "I am really deeply worried. You can't pay me for that little article—a 'scrid' we would call it in Maine.... Now I'm an honest woman, if not a good one, and I can't countenance such business methods. I accept on only one condition, that I do another scrid for absolutely nothing except good wishes."

In the spring of 1964 Lunt and George Stevens of Lippincott asked Chase to collaborate with Robert Ballou on an abridgment of the Bible. She refused since she disdained condensed Bibles and loathed the Revised Standard Version, which she considered "merely another paraphrase." At least, she thought, the Authorized Version was a work of art, which the Revised was not. She said she would do almost anything for Lunt, but she could not praise the RSV and maintain her integrity.

Although by the mid-1960s Chase's intellectual vigor was on the wane, her books continued to delight and please. One of her ardent admirers was Hugh Stalker, a wealthy and erudite physician from Grosse Pointe, Michigan. He was introduced to her works in 1940 when he read *A Goodly Fellowship*; he was so moved by it that he sent her his copy to be signed. When she returned the autographed book, she enclosed a note saying that the autobiography "seemed very simple to me when I wrote it. ... I have been amazed at the friends it has made, none more sincere and kindly than yourself."

Among these friends was Sister Mary Gratia, a nun at the Dominican College of San Rafael in California. Sister Mary read *A Goodly Fellowship* aloud to her colleagues and wrote Chase that she "felt a tinge of sadness when the [book ended]. I am sure all the others felt the same way. Many an evening at recreation we discussed . . . with gaiety, or earnestness, your adventures in the teaching profession. It is a sound book, a merry book, a lovely book! We were respectful of all that was asked of you at Buck's Harbor, we rocked with discreet laughter over your hazards in Chicago and your experiences at Mrs. Moffat's; we relished and admired all that happened to you at the Hillside School; we were delighted to learn that you were so happy at St. Catherine's and that you enjoyed such 'goodly fellowship' at Smith. This is just to let you know what a 'goodly' impact your book has made on our community."

The Stalker-Chase correspondence, comprising about seventy-five letters, spans a period of nearly ten years, from January 1960 to December 1969. Chase's response to the doctor's fan mail expressed her effusive but genuine sense of gratitude for his magnanimity. He sent her gifts of every description: poinsettias for Christmas, Easter lilies, colorful quilts, embossed treasure boxes, Bristol Cream sherry, assorted French delicacies, and exotic confections.

When Stalker read *The Lovely Ambition*, he was deeply touched. The book gave him "once again a breath of the Maine pines," and he wrote Chase thanking her for sharing childhood memories. He said that it was refreshing to read about a closely knit family, embracing their joys and sorrows, when most writers were composing lurid novels filled with violence, lust, and murder. He noted that there must be many readers who were indebted to her for her "flowing English in which one can lose time and even thoughts of the outside world."

In 1965 Chase sent Stalker a copy of *The Story of Lighthouses* as a slight token of appreciation. The benevolent doctor's largess prompted Duckett to voice her personal thanks:

"You do not know me, but I feel that you are a wonderful friend of Mary's, and I share in the joy which your delightful gifts have brought to this home . . . we are looking every day at the extraordinary beauty of the amaryllis—the colors and the richness of its great flowers dominate our living room. . . . "

When Chase returned from England in March 1964, after a long bout with bronchitis, she was greeted by Stalker's gift, a magnificent white azalea tree. She told him that "your white tree is here and Holy Week . . . is joyous and gay, thanks to you. Why you should be so kind to me, I wouldn't have the remotest idea, but I am thrilled and most grateful. . . . "

Chase's frequent attacks of bronchitis and progressive difficulty in breathing were the first symptoms of emphysema. She gave up smoking, which she confessed was as great a sacrifice as Abraham's offering of his son, Isaac. But she continued writing and composed four engaging childrens' books: *Richard Mansfield* (1962), *Dolly Moses* (1963), *Victoria: A Pig in a Pram* (1963), and *A Walk on an Iceberg* (1966). She wrote Mathilde that she liked "Victoria" better than anything she had ever done: "It's a bit useless and funny and a bit gay and sad, just a short thing."

Lunt told Chase that "Dolly Moses is just perfect. The iceberg and lighthouses are books apart. Dolly Moses belongs with Victoria and Richard Mansfield. My affection for those two is about equal, but Dolly noses them out." In one of his last recorded letters to Chase, North complimented her on this story: "It is so rich and rewarding, so full of warm memories of another era and sharp vignettes of your lovely mother, your somewhat less discerning father, and your beloved Aunt Sophie. . . . This is definitely a read aloud book for the whole family from nine to ninety."

Between 1962 and 1965 Chase signed contracts for five books and sent rough drafts to McGraw Hill for the first two. She had so many obligations that she could not remember what she had promised to write. She had an agreement with E.P. Dutton for an account of her teaching experiences, three

more with McGraw Hill for "Portraits from the Old Testament," a piece on "King Saul and His Times," and "Constancy,
Queen of Cows." The fifth, "This I Have Loved," to be published by Macmillan, would be a 125,000 word reminiscence
for which she would receive a $10,000 advance. She also
planned another book for Norton on "Sarah Orne Jewett as a
Social Historian."

Chase was among the few critics who accepted Cather's
assessment that The Country of the Pointed Firs was one of three
American works most likely to achieve permanent recognition.
In 1962 Chase contributed an essay to David Bonnell Green's
volume, The World of Dunnet Landing: A Sarah Orne Jewett
Collection (University of Nebraska Press). She maintained that
Jewett's creations of close study and sensitive imagination were
timeless. She cited some characters in "Pointed Firs," Captain
Littlefield, Almira Todd, Joanna Burden: "Their immortality is
enhanced because the seemingly frail manner of their portrayal
. . . allows their truth to reveal itself more clearly . . . She has
been deservedly praised for the taut and beautiful simplicity of
her style, for her sympathetic humor, for her remarkable gift of
making the ordinary dramatic, of enlightening the common-
place. . . . In describing persons and places with accuracy and
affection, she recorded the roots of their lives, the sources of
their speech, the contributions made by them in the story of a
nation."

Chase's last three published works were A Journey to Boston
(1965); A Walk on an Iceberg (1966) and the introduction to
the Norton edition of Jewett's stories (1968, reissued in 1982).
A Journey to Boston was a tribute to her many acquaintances of
Polish origin. It was a brief work with a frail plot and a bland
cast of characters, a feeble endeavor which most of her friends
regarded as a mistake. But many reviewers praised the novel. In
the Omaha (Nebraska) Sunday World Herald Magazine Books of
the Week (March 28, 1965), the critic observed: "A tragedy,
cameo-style. There is not a word wasted . . . It has the warm

glow of fine old pewter and, for all its brevity, it says a great deal about Americans and the American way of life. As I write this I keep thinking of Willa Cather and her Nebraskan novels. In the way she drew on her knowledge of . . . the Bohemians of this state, so Miss Chase has drawn on Connecticut's Polish Americans."

In her penultimate story, *A Walk on an Iceberg*, Chase recounted a tale told by her grandmother Eliza. She thought this lady was "really something, terribly attractive, even when at 87 she left this world, with her own teeth and her eyes bright as ever." The book is dedicated to the memory of that remarkable woman who discovered early on that "almost everything that matters most in life can be found within the covers of books." In 1967 Robert Cross, secretary of Bowdoin's Alumni Fund, informed Chase that *A Walk on an Iceberg* would be placed in a special collection of volumes written by or about Bowdoin alumni, honor graduates and faculty members.

Chase's last achievement was the editing of a compilation of Jewett's stories. In her introduction she purposely identified Jewett with the coast of Maine, for that state is widely recognized as the country of the pointed firs, and Jewett was inextricably bound to it. Chase noted that Jewett's rare sensitivity "sets [her] apart not only from all other Maine writers, but from many, if not most writers of all time . . . , gives her an enviable stature, makes her . . . the deeply desired, if unreachable model for us all." In Chase's obituary, the *Portland* (Maine) *Press Herald*, commented: "Miss Chase has succeeded her childhood idol, Sarah Orne Jewett, as first among literary ladies of her generation."

Toward the end of her fruitful life, Chase discovered the greatest consolation in works by Plato and Pericles, Virginia Woolf, and in Cather's lovely novels. She believed that in books there were men of greater stature than in life. This poignant epitaph written by Alcuin, an eighteenth-century monk, haunted her through all her days:

Alcuin was my name,
Busy as you are, don't hurry by,
Please! Stop for a moment,
Read what I wrote for you when
I once lived among you:
"Learn how men can live by
Words set down in order."

The classics and the Old Testament seemed to be a collision of worlds in the turbulent decade of the sixties, but they continued to be Chase's mainstay. She avoided reading newspapers, except for the *New York Times Book Review* section, and she refused to buy a television set, for the world was too much with her as it was. She became an advocate of Bertrand Russell. She considered that "we've destroyed quite enough as it is and I'm for saving what we have left, though it isn't much."

In 1966 Chase and Duckett went to England for six months, their final trip abroad. They sailed on the *Sylvania*, a small Cunarder with a congenial crew and an outstanding library. From April to mid-August Chase was in a Cambridge hospital with shingles, "the most horrid of diseases and the most tenacious." In March 1967 Duckett broke her hip, and although she had excellent care, Chase worried about her constantly. Chase was experiencing further physical problems: shortly after her eighty-first birthday she tripped on the living room rug, sustaining three fractured ribs and a sprained right arm.

Chase's letters, usually brimming with optimism, began to assume somber tones of disillusionment, despair, and remorse. She wrote Mildred that she hated the dark, short New England days. They were darker and shorter in England, but the lights of Queen's College shone across the river; and the river, cascading through the weir, was strangely comforting. She said she kept writing, since she felt better when she was working. Despite the fact that she was aware of her limitations, she was not quite ready to admit that she had lost her magic touch with the pen.

Chase did not like growing old, anxious, and ill. She began to withdraw from the battlefield of life, for she found it easier to surrender than to struggle. She reread Thoreau and noted that he "says he is on his way to a 'fairer country.' I wish I had his faith, but I don't. At the moment I'm not too close on my way to any country, fair or otherwise."

In those dark days Chase was fortified by her steadfast devotion to the church. She still "[praised] the Lord of Hosts with good reason and agree with old Anselm that faith is a means to knowledge rather than knowledge as a means to faith. . . . I still think that, once one sees all the stumbling blocks in the church as of human creation, and understands that ignorance, superstition and pitiful egoism have placed them there through the centuries, it can still make the crooked straight, and the rough places plain, the blind see and the lame walk once more. I love it still, with a great love and it does not fail me."

In December 1967 President Mendenhall announced the trustees' decision to designate two buildings in honor of the two women who had served Smith faithfully throughout the years. Mary Ellen Chase House and Eleanor S. Duckett House became the property of the college when the Burnham School merged with Stoneleigh Prospect. It was anticipated that each dormitory would accommodate approximately fifty students.

From late 1968 to 1971 there was no contact from Chase to her Minnesota friends. On February 11, 1972, Mathilde wrote Mildred this note: "Herewith a rather cool, rather detached letter from Eleanor Duckett. I had just reread Mary's book about Abby Aldrich Rockefeller and that was my excuse for attempting some sort of communication once again. And you can see with what a sad result."

Mathilde may have considered this message dispassionate, but Duckett's account of Chase's final illness was a heartrending commentary on the depleted quality of her friend's life. It revealed a reserved English woman's way of imparting her own feelings of profound grief and loss. This frail, inarticulate woman lying defenselessly in bed was not the vibrant Mary Chase whom Duckett had known for forty-five years, but a pitiful invalid who could only squeeze her hand as a gesture of affection. The saddest aspect of her condition was the dissolution of a once brilliant mind.

Duckett's letter was written on February 1, 1972. "I am writing for Mary. For nearly three years she has been ill in hospital and six months in the Pine Rest Nursing Home. I have been alone in this house for nearly three years. She has emphysema and she has gradually become worse. Now she cannot carry on a conversation, she is afraid of people she does not recognize, and she hardly talks at all. She cannot walk, though once or twice a day she is put into the easy chair beside her bed for lunch or supper. She sleeps a good deal, but constantly she finds difficulty in breathing. She lies in bed or sits in her chair, silent for most of the time. I go to visit her when I can, but it is hard to see Mary, once so full of life, lying there helpless and voiceless. The doctor says she may live for months. She cannot read and she takes no interest in what is going on outside in the world. It is tragic. . . . The Pine Rest Nursing Home has very kind and devoted nurses, but there is, as in most nursing homes, an air of silence and helplessness about the place, patients lying prone in bed, or trying to walk, with no great cheer, for most of them will not recover. I am sorry to tell you this, and please don't write to tell Mary that I have written of her tragic fate. It is dreadful to think of Mary as she once was and now is. . . . I am well and very busy, working for the church and on a book. If you ever come here you could see Mary, but you would not get her talking to you. She remembers people, but can't communicate. I am sorry to write all this, but you wanted to know, of course. With my sympathy as I know that this will hurt you. I encourage people to go and see her, for that revives her for a time."

Mary Ellen Chase died on July 28, 1973. She slipped away peacefully, in no great pain. A graveside funeral was held in

Blue Hill three days later. At her memorial service in St. John's Church Duckett spoke, sharing some vivid anecdotes about her friend. Those who attended commented that the tribute was especially striking since it conveyed a true sense of Chase's immortality.

After Chase's death Duckett's colleagues noticed an abrupt change in her personality. At first she attempted to emulate her late companion but, as time elapsed, she became more outgoing and self-reliant and seemed to enjoy her freedom. She gave up the Paradise Road home and rented a small apartment in Northampton. She became immersed in the activities at St. John's, attending services at least four times a week and was appointed one of the first female lay members of the congregation. Fellow parishioners observed that she was "golden in her actions," exceptional in her work with the Youth Group. In 1973, at age ninety-three, she reluctantly entered the Pine Rest Nursing Home where she died three years later.

Chase and Duckett are interred next to each other in Blue Hill's charming old graveyard that overlooks the mountains and the surrounding bay. Their original intention was to be buried on Windswept grounds and they had fashioned a gravestone at the cliff's edge. Duckett's humble grave has three words on the tombstone: "Dona Nobis Pacem." Chase's marker is of Blue Hill granite with a Saxon cross atop it; it bears her favorite passage from Isaiah 40: "And they shall mount up with wings as eagles." The juxtaposition of their graves indicates Duckett's importance to Chase and her willingness to reveal their intimacy.

Duckett's site belonged rightfully to Edith Chase Weren. But Chase upstaged her sibling. In her will she stipulated that, should Duckett die in this country she would be buried alongside the Chase family. When Edith was informed of this startling provision, she gasped and exclaimed: "Mary has won again!" She then took to her bed. Three weeks after her sister's death, Edith had a fatal heart attack. Edith's tiny headstone, situated in an obscure corner of the plot, is identified only by her initials and the date of death.

In her fiction Chase often endowed her characters with visionary powers: the redoubtable Sarah Holt, who cast a spell on everyone she knew; *Windswept*'s irresistible Ann Marston, standing at the edge of a brave new world. Ann was a woman of rare gifts who could see beyond the ordinary, beyond her own personal gratification. She was waiting and ready for a world bequeathed through the perseverance of her forebears. Like her creator, Ann had an unbreakable optimism and a deep understanding of the human heart. Her world was shaped by the beauty around her: the lovely Maine countryside, the seashore, red berries in the tangled grass. "If faith were gone, the old, simple faith in a design for one's life, not forged on earth by oneself, but framed in Heaven, one could, if one would, build one's own design through an awakened consciousness even of material things, the visible and the temporal holding within themselves the means to the invisible and eternal. One can . . . rise to life immortal . . . one can find the golden branch among the shadows."

Bibliography

BOOKS

His Birthday, Boston: Pilgrim Press, 1915.

The Girl From The Big Horn Country, Boston: Page Co., 1916.

Virginia Of Elk Creek Valley, Boston: Page Co., 1917.

The Art of Narration (with Frances K. Del Plaine), New York: F.S. Crofts & Co., 1926.

Mary Christmas, Boston: Little Brown & Co., 1926.

Thomas Hardy from Serial to Novel, Ph.D. dissertation, University of Minnesota Press, 1927.

Uplands, Boston: Little Brown & Co., 1927.

The Writing of Informal Essays (with Margaret Eliot Macgregor), New York: Henry Holt & Co., 1928.

The Golden Asse & Other Essays, Henry Holt & Co., 1929.

Constructive Theme Writing for College Freshmen, New York: Henry Holt & Co., 1929.

The Silver Shell, New York: Henry Holt & Co., 1930.

A Goodly Heritage, Henry Holt & Co., 1932; new edition, Avon, 1957.

Mary Peters, Macmillan, 1934.

Silas Crockett, Macmillan, 1935.

This England, Macmillan, 1936 (*As In England*, London: Collins, 1937).

Dawn in Lyonesse, Macmillan, 1938.

A Goodly Fellowship, Macmillan, 1939; Collins, 1940; reprinted by Bantam, 1957; reissued in paper by Macmillan, 1960.

Windswept, Macmillan, 1941; Collins, 1942.

The Bible and The Common Reader, Macmillan, 1944; revised edition 1952.

Jonathan Fisher: Maine Parson 1768-1847, Macmillan, 1948.

The Plum Tree, Macmillan, 1949; Collins, 1950.

Abby Aldrich Rockefeller, Macmillan, 1950.

Readings from the Bible, Macmillan, 1952.

Recipe for a Magic Childhood, Macmillan, 1952.

The White Gate, New York: W.W. Norton & Co., 1954.

Life and Language in the Old Testament, Norton, 1955; Collins, 1956.

The Edge of Darkness, Norton, 1957; Collins, 1958; People's Book Club, Family Book Club, and Abridged Books, 1958.

Sailing the Seven Seas, Boston: Houghton Mifflin, 1958.

Donald McKay and the Clipper Ships, Houghton Mifflin, 1959.

The Lovely Ambition, Norton, 1960; Collins, 1961.

The Fishing Fleets of New England, Houghton Mifflin, 1961.

The Psalms for the Common Reader, Norton, 1962.

The Prophets for the Common Reader, Norton, 1963.

Victoria, A Pig in a Pram, Norton, 1963.

A Journey to Boston, Norton, 1965.

The Story of Lighthouses, Norton, 1965.

A Walk on an Iceberg, Norton, 1966.

SHORT STORIES *(partial list)*

How Four Girls 'Discovered' Maine, *Ladies Home Journal*, May 1917.

A Return to Constancy, *Harper's*, November 1918, reprinted in *Woman's Day*, June 1944.

Marigolds, *Harper's*, May 1919; reprinted in *Woman's Day*, June 1944.

Sure Dwellings, *Harper's*, November 1919; reprinted in *Woman's Day*, June 1944.

The Waste of the Ointment, *Pictorial Review*, July 1921.

Upland Pastures, *Atlantic Monthly*, May 1922.

The Garment of Praise, *Scribner's*, October 1925; translated as "Le Manteau de Louange" in *La Nouvelle Semaine Artistique et Littéraire*, March 31 and April 7, 1928.

Salesmanship, first prize chosen from 11,000 applicants, $2500, *Pictorial Review*, July 1930; reprinted in *Scholastic*, April 17, 1937.

Mrs. Gowan Gives Notice, *Atlantic*, May 1932.

Mrs. Penlust on the Damascus Road, *Atlantic*, October 1932.

A Pinch of Snuff, *North American Review*, June 1935; reprinted in *Woman's Day*, February 1943.

Taxi Driver 63, *Delineator*, February 1936.

The Golden Age, *North American Review*, March 1936.

A Candle at Night, *Collier's*, May 9, 1942.

Honeymoon 1854, *Woman's Day*, June 1954.

ARTICLES IN PERIODICALS AND NEWSPAPERS

The Islands Lose a Friend, *Outlook*, February 21, 1923.

A Kitchen Parnassus, *Atlantic*, August 1926.

The Golden Asse-A Tribute, *Atlantic*, February 1927.

The Saints in Maine, *Commonweal*, May 25, 1927.

Mystical Mathematicks, *Commonweal*, January 25, 1928.

Not in Cadiz, *North American Review*, May 1928.

Wormwood for Thoughts, *Atlantic*, May, 1928.

Have you Martin Chuzzlewit? *Atlantic*, September 1928.

On Kitchens and Cloisters, *Commonweal*, September 12, 1928.

Concerning Old Things and New, *House Beautiful*, January 1931.

She's Had the Doctor!, *Atlantic*, June 1933.

Confidences of a Lecturer, *Commonweal*, May 26, 1933.

The Dean of American Essayists, *Commonweal*, August 18, 1933.

The American Father Attends his Wife's Reunion, *Scribner's*, July 1934.

What Do You Expect of College for Your Daughter? *Ladies Home Journal*, August 1936.

The Abundant Life in Books, *Ladies Home Journal*, September 1936.

Are Parents Afraid of Their Children? *Ladies Home Journal*, March 1937.

An Unpopular Suggestion, *The Writer*, April 1937.

Old Time Christmases in Maine, *Ladies Home Journal*, December 1937; *Reader's Digest*, January 1938.

Rather Late for Christmas, *Vogue*, December 1, 1938; as "Christmas Is a State of Mind," *Reader's Digest*, January 1938; in *Vogue's First Reader*; in *Literary Cavalcade*, December 1949.

I Like the Younger Generation, *Ladies Home Journal*, December 1939.

Our Educational Heritage, *American Association of University Women Journal*, January 1940.

Time to Oneself, *Yale Review*, September 1940; as "You Become Someone-Alone," *Reader's Digest*, October 1940.

Head and Hands Working Together, *Common Ground*, Autumn 1940.

Progressive Education, *New York Times Magazine*, February 9, 1941.

When You Go to England, *Harper's*, August 1941.

An Ancient Democracy in a Modern, *Common Ground*, Winter 1943.

Early Reading of the Bible, *National Parent Teacher*, May 1945.

Are We Afraid to be Alone?, *Woman's Day*, October 1949.

Sorry, We Can't Afford It, *Good Housekeeping*, November 1950.

Recipe for a Magic Childhood, *Ladies Home Journal*, May 1951.

Must America Live in Fear? *Coronet*, July 1953.

A Legacy from my Childhood, *Parents*, August 1953.

The Virtue of Living Fully, *House and Garden*, September 1953.

If I Were Your Age, *Glamour*, March 1954.

What Has Happened to Common Sense? *Coronet*, May 1954; *Reader's Digest*, July 1954.

In Praise of American Hands, *Glamour*, October 1954.
The Bible in Our Kitchen, *Woman's Day*, November 1954.
Courtesy on Wheels, *Atlantic*, October 1956.
She Misses Some Goals, *Life*, December 24, 1956.
Half a Dollar or Huckleberry Finn? *New York Herald Tribune* Book Review, April 3, 1960.
My Novels About Maine, *Colby Library Quarterly*, March 1962.

CONTRIBUTIONS TO BOOKS

"The Influence of the King James Bible on Two Great Masters of 19th Century Prose," in M.B. Crook, ed., *The Bible and Its Literary Associations*, Nashville: Abington Press, 1937.
"The Teaching of English," in R.M. Gay, ed., *Essays on the Teaching of English*, Cambridge: Harvard University Press, 1940.
Preface to the Book of Job, New York: Limited Editions Club, 1940.
"New England: Land of God," in *Look at the U.S.A.*, Boston: Houghton Mifflin & Co., 1947.
Preface to The Book of Ruth, New York: Limited Editions Club, 1948.
Introduction to Thomas Hardy, *Far From the Madding Crowd*, New York: Dutton, 1951; Everyman's Library Edition.
"Our Goodly Heritage," *The Northampton Book*, edited and published by the Tercentenary Committee, Northampton Mass., 1954.
"On Teaching and Teachers" in D. Louise Sharp, ed., *Why Teach?* New York: Henry Holt & Co., 1957.
Introduction to Henry Fielding, *Joseph Andrews*, New York: W.W. Norton, 1958; The Norton Library Edition.
Introduction to *The Country of the Pointed Firs & Other Stories*, Norton Edition, 1968; paper, 1982.

SECONDARY MATERIAL

Chase, Evelyn Hyman. *Feminist Convert: A Portrait of Mary Ellen Chase*. Santa Barbara: John Daniel and Co., 1988.
Westbrook, Perry. *Mary Ellen Chase*. New York: Twayne Publishers, 1965.